The Textual Condition

**PRINCETON STUDIES IN
CULTURE / POWER / HISTORY**

The Textual Condition

JEROME J. McGANN

PRINCETON UNIVERSITY PRESS

PRINCETON, NEW JERSEY

Library of Congress Cataloging-in-Publication Data

McGann, Jerome J.
The textual condition / Jerome J. McGann
p. cm. — (Princeton studies in culture/power/history)
Includes bibliographical references and index.
ISBN 0-691-06931-X — 0-691-01518-X (pbk.)
1. English literature—Criticism, Textual.   2. American
literature—Criticism, Textual.   3. English literature—History and
criticism—Theory, etc.   4. American literature—History and
criticism—Theory, etc.   5. Pound, Ezra, 1885-1972—Criticism,
Textual.   6. Transmission of texts.   7. Criticism, Textual.
8. Editing.   I. Title.   II. Series.
PR21.M37 1991
801'.959—dc20   91-16996 CIP

This book has been composed in Linotron Sabon and Helvetica

Princeton University Press books are printed on acid-free paper and meet the
guidelines for permanence and durability of the Committee on
Production Guidelines for Book Longevity
of the Council on Library Resources

Printed in the United States of America

1   3   5   7   9   10   8   6   4   2

1   3   5   7   9   10   8   6   4   2
(Pbk.)

FOR VIRGIL

The eyes of fire, the nostrils of air,
the mouth of water, the beard
of earth.

You can't have art without

resistance in the material.

—*William Morris*

Contents

Illustrations

Preface

CHAPTERS 4, 5, and the conclusion were first written and delivered as lectures. I have restyled chapter 5 and the conclusion for the conventions of book presentation. Because the argument of chapter 4 is so closely tied to the form of the text's first presentation, I have kept the signs of its original textuality. The contradiction which necessarily appears when one reads this text in its bookish form is, however, a positive virtue, so far as the general argument of this book is concerned.

Chapters 6 and 7, as well as the introduction and conclusion appear in print for the first time here. Chapters 1, 2, and 3 have appeared in much abbreviated forms in the following publications: *Devils and Angels: Textual Editing and Literary Theory*, ed. Phillip Cohen (Charlottesville: University Press of Virginia, 1991); *Text 5* (1991); *Documentary Editing* 12 (September 1990): 56–61. Chapter 4 was previously printed in *Text* 4 (1988); chapter 5 in *The Library Chronicle of the University of Texas at Austin* 20 (1990): 13–37.

I am grateful to the New Directions Corporation and The William Blake Trust for giving permission to reproduce various illustrations included here.

For help of so many kinds I wish to thank in particular Charles Bernstein, Nick Dirks, Robert Essick, David Greetham, Susan Howe, Steve McCaffery, Randall McLeod, Marjorie Perloff, Lawrence Rainey, Jeffrey Skoblow, and my friends at the University of Texas at Austin and Texas A&M University. Also, the Center for Advanced Studies, University of Virginia, provided me with time and money, for which special thanks are due to Paul Gross, Hugh Kelly, and Dexter Whitehead.

Finally, and first of all, there is Virgil Burnett, that master of unnam'd forms who first opened my eyes to these and other things many years ago.

The Textual Condition

Texts and Textualities

BOTH THE PRACTICE and the study of human culture comprise a network of symbolic exchanges. Because human beings are not angels, these exchanges always involve material negotiations. Even in their most complex and advanced forms—when the negotiations are carried out as textual events—the intercourse that is being human is materially executed: as spoken texts or scripted forms. To participate in these exchanges is to have entered what I wish to call here "the textual condition."

The sexual event itself—which is, as the poets have always known, a model of the textual condition—involves far more than the intercourse of reproductive organs. The climactic marriage of our persons is most completely experienced as a total body sensation almost mystical in its intensity as in its meaning. In those moments we realize (in both senses of the word) that to be human is to be involved with another, and ultimately with many others. Beyond that great and strange experience of immediacy the sexual event organizes a vast network of related acts of intercourse at the personal as well as more extended social levels: courtship rituals, domestic economies, political exchanges, and so forth. All of these activities take multiple particular forms. Love, even romantic love, is a social event, as *Romeo and Juliet* or *Werther* will always remind us. As such, love is and has ever been one of the great scenes of textuality.

These elective affinities between love and textuality exist because love and text are two of our most fundamental social acts. We make love and we make texts, and we make both in a seemingly endless series of imaginative variations.

This book is an inquiry into the nature of texts and textuality. The inquiry is grounded in the thought that texts represent—are in themselves—certain kinds of human acts. This idea may appear so unexceptionable as to stand beyond the need of dispute, perhaps even beyond the need of elaboration. But our culture's now dominant conceptions of textuality are in fact very different. Today, texts are largely imagined as scenes of reading rather than scenes of writing. This "readerly" view of text has been most completely elaborated through the modern hermeneutical tradition in which text is not something we *make* but something we *interpret*. The difference from the approach taken in the present study is crucial.

"Well, of course texts are written—or spoken. No one denies that. But texts have to be read in order to be understood. Textuality is a scene in which readers respond to the texts they encounter. If one locates the reader at the center of textuality, it is because the text is passive and silent, because it needs the reader's activity to infuse it with meaning, to bring it back to life."

"So reading is a textual activity."

"Most definitely."

"But tell me, when and where—and how—does the activity of reading take place? Is it an affair of the mind alone, of the individual standing silent before the mute text, building invisible cities of meaning to unheard melodies of truth? If so, how do we engage with those secret interior texts—if in fact we can call them texts at all?"

Reading appears always and only as text, in one or another physically determinate and socially determined form. This is not to deny either the reality or the importance of silent and individual reading. It is merely to say that textuality cannot

4

be understood except as a phenomenal event, and that reading itself can only be understood when it has assumed specific
material constitutions. Silence before a text is neither our best
nor our oldest model of textuality. Indeed, insofar as it is a
textual model at all, it has been licensed by another (prior)
model altogether.

II

Critical interpreters of text—in this tradition, Paul De Man
is an exemplary figure—observe a very special scene of textuality:

> Prior to any generalization about literature, literary texts have
> to be read, and the possibility of reading can never be taken
> for granted. It is an act of understanding that can never be
> observed, nor in any way prescribed or verified. A literary text
> is not a phenomenal event that can be granted any form of
> positive existence, whether as a fact of nature or as an act of
> the mind.[1]

This is De Man's version of the Shelleyan lament: "When
composition begins, inspiration is already on the decline." It
is the source of his now-celebrated elegiac reading of the textual condition, which he observes as the reader's pursuit of a
meaning or closure in perpetual retreat beyond the horizon of
the reader's visions.

But if Demannic reading is "an act of understanding that
can never be observed. . .or verified," the texts embodying
those acts of understanding *have* been observed and verified,
elaborated and contested. In this crucial and fundamental
sense De Man's own "acts of mind" have taken on various
forms of "positive existence." As such they too have entered
the textual condition—that scene of complex dialogue and
interchange, of testing and texting.

De Man's project as a theorist of texts centered in his fun-

5

damental argument with empirical and positivist traditions of philology and criticism. De Man argued that an error ran through those traditions. This error took its origin in the scholar's faith that disciplines of knowledge could arrive at textual realities, could bring substantial truth to literary studies. De Man labored to show the illusions involved in any project that believed it could close, even for a moment, the hermeneutic circle.

The force of De Man's critique of criticism was somewhat deflected when it was pointed out—for example, by Paul Bové—that De Man's struggle may have been with a phantom of his own making.[2] New Criticism was a paradigm target of De Man's attack, but Bové had no difficulty in showing that this hermeneutical movement was already fully aware of the *aporias* of reading and the instabilities of the interpreter's text.

In fact, the textual *aporias* that emerge through reading and hermeneutics are a function of the peculiar textual model these traditions tend to work with. This textual model—which is as much the object of Stanley Fish as of Paul De Man, of Roland Barthes as of Cleanth Brooks—is sketched in the passage from De Man which I have already cited. It is a model in which there is only one agent, the solitary "reader," whose pursuit of meaning involves an activity of ceaseless metaphoric production. These metaphoric constructs are the reader's "insights" into the meaning he desires. For the traditional interpreter, the constructs re-present a version or vision of the Truth, one that is more or less adequate, more or less exemplary. For the deconstructive reader, the visions are, with respect to the ideal of Truth, simply different styles of failure. The "truth" they reveal is the special form of blindness to which a particular reader is prone.

What is important to note is the homologous models of textuality which operate in each of these versions of the interpretive scene. In deconstructing the *aporias* of the interpreters, De Man becomes what he beholds. This homology appears most dramatically if we turn to the textual model which evolved through, and finally came to dominate, the most empirical and positivist traditions of modern philology. A great gulf is assumed to stand between those seekers after "fact and reason," the scholars, and those seekers after "wisdom and insight," the interpreters. In fact, both assume the same model of reading, and both share an experience of loss and inadequacy in the face of their critical objects. De Man's elegiac vision is echoed by the textual scholar G. Thomas Tanselle in his recent set of philosophical reflections on editing and textual scholarship, *A Rationale of Textual Criticism* (1989):

> What every artifact displays is the residue of an unequal contest: the effort of a human being to transcend the human, an effort constantly thwarted by physical realities. Even a document with a text of the sort not generally regarded as art—a simple message to a friend, for example—illustrates the immutable condition of written statements: in writing down a message, one brings down an abstraction to the concrete, where it is an alien, damaged here and there through the intractability of the physical.[3]

Tanselle and De Man, in other respects so different, come together as textual idealists. Each is caught in his own version of an impossible dialectic, an "unequal contest" between transphenomenal desires and factive, material conditions. Each pivots between, on one side, a Urizenic demand for a transcendence of the human:

> I have sought for a joy without pain,
> For a solid without fluctuation.
>
> > *(The Book of Urizen* pl. 4)

and, on the other, a romantic reciprocal—a lament that the terms of such a demand can never be met:

7

When composition begins, inspiration is already on the decline, and the most glorious poetry that has ever been communicated to the world is probably a feeble shadow of the original conception of the poet.[4]

Between these two imaginative worlds the life of this textual
model hovers, like a dark star. De Man calls this star "the
void"; Tanselle calls it "the intractability of the physical."

There is another way of thinking about texts. According to
this other way, the study of texts begins with readings of the
texts, as De Man says; but those readings—like the texts
which stand before them—are materially and socially defined. The readings, as Derrida has shown, are structured
philosophically—and historically actuated—as writings. According to this view, the physical embodiment of text is not
in itself the sign that text has been "damaged," or that we
have entered a world of "intractable" materialities and temporal *aporias*. Notions of perfection need not be derived
from abstractions; indeed, there are many—Blake and Byron
come immediately to mind—who have believed that models
grounded in ideal forms originate such notions of damage,
void, and the intractability of the physical. In this humanist
perspective one will speak of the "perfection" of a certain
poem (say, Keats's "La Belle Dame Sans Merci," Dickinson's
"Because I Could Not Stop for Death"), or of a certain individual (Sister Teresa, Michael Jordan, Marilyn Monroe), and
so forth. Each of these examples reminds us that perfection
exists, but always within limits:

> Love in full life and length, not love ideal,
>> No, nor ideal beauty, that fine name,
> But something better still, so very real,
>> That the sweet model must have been the same.
>
> (Byron, *Beppo* st. 13)

Such figures are models of perfection within sets of terms that
they themselves make visible and define. Their perfection is

not abstract and general but concrete and particular. It is a function of the specific world(s) in which they live and move and have their being.[5]

These are figures, as it were, of perfect limitation. The reality of their perfectness, however, if it is to be understood, must be sharply located within the sociohistorical particularities which the perfection defines. None of these figures are "universally" perfect; each displays perfection within a concrete set of determinants that have different spatial and temporal coordinates.[6] (It is necessary, in fact, that their constitutions be able to be seen as limited, perhaps even imperfect, if approached from different perspectives.)

When we imagine the textual condition within this horizon, a world appears that is very different from the one viewed by De Man and Tanselle. This world comes into focus when we ask James McLaverty's provocative question: "If the *Mona Lisa* is in the Louvre in Paris, where is *Hamlet*?[7] In this world, time, space, and physicality are not the emblems of a fall from grace, but the bounding conditions which turn gracefulness abounding. It is equally a world where the many departures from grace—our damaged orders and beings— appear in correspondingly determinate forms.

The textual condition's only immutable law is the law of change. It is a law, however, like all laws, that operates within certain limits. Every text enters the world under determinate sociohistorical conditions, and while these conditions may and should be variously defined and imagined, they establish the horizon within which the life histories of different texts can play themselves out. The law of change declares that these histories will exhibit a ceaseless process of textual development and mutation—a process which can only be arrested if all the textual transformations of a particular work fall into nonexistence. To study texts and textualities, then, we have to study these complex (and open-ended) histories of textual change and variance.

But texts do not simply vary over time. Texts vary from

themselves (as it were) immediately, as soon as they engage with the readers they anticipate. Two persons see "the same" movie or read "the same" book and come away with quite different understandings of what they saw or read. Do not imagine that these variations are a simple function of differentials that reside "in the readers": in personal differences, or in differences of class, gender, social, and geographical circumstances. The differences arise from variables that will be found on both sides of the textual transaction: "in" the texts themselves, and "in" the readers of the texts. The texts themselves (so-called) can always be shown to have been underdetermined with respect to their possible meanings. This happens because language can only exist in a textual condition of some sort, and because that condition—the embodiment of language—releases the Idea of Language (which is an imagination of codes and rules) into a more or less Chaotic Order.[8]

Every text has variants of itself screaming to get out, or antithetical texts waiting to make themselves known. These variants and antitheses appear (and multiply) over time, as the hidden features of the textual media are developed and made explicit. They appear because even the most "informational" text comprises an interactive mechanism of communicative exchange. Various readers and audiences are hidden in our texts, and the traces of their multiple presence are scripted at the most material levels.

III

One kind of text takes this complex human event for its special subject: poetry, or imaginative writing in general. The object of poetry is to display the textual condition. Poetry is language that calls attention to itself, that takes its own textual activities as its ground subject. To say this is not at all to say that poetic texts lack polemical, moral, or ideological materials and functions. The practice of language takes place within those domains. But poetical texts operate to display their own practices, to put them forward as the subject of attention. That means, necessarily, that poetical texts—unlike propaganda and advertising texts, which are also highly self-conscious constructions—turn readers back upon themselves, make them attentive to what they are doing when they read.

Poetical texts must be, in this respect, sharply distinguished from texts that have imagined themselves as informational— texts that have been constructed on a sender/receiver, or transmissional, model. Literary texts, by contrast, are paradigms of those interactive and feedback mechanisms that Humberto Maturana and Francisco Varela have studied as, and called, autopoiesis.[9] In a vehicular textual model, by contrast, the textual paradigm is one which does not interfere with or "distort" a message. The vehicle of transmission is thereby sharply distinguished from its "message," and textual study devotes itself in the main to the pursuit of channels (and the *idea* of channels) that are free from noise. (When hermeneutics operates from such a theory of the text, the informational message is called "meaning.")

Literary texts may be—have often been—studied according to these kinds of informational models. But the literary text does not easily submit to them. There is (to parody the now-famous formulation of Wellek and Warren) a "Mode of *Resistance* in the Literary Work." The resistance appears as the work's patent designs of self-attention, the many ways it turns into itself (in both senses of "into"). Textual scholars register these forms of self-attention as the inseparability of the medium and the message, the advent of meaning as a material event which is coterminous (in several senses) with its textual execution. Literary works do not know themselves, and cannot *be* known, apart from their specific material modes of existence/resistance. They are not channels of transmission, they are particular forms of transmissive interaction.

A study of textuality grounded in paleography, bibliography, and the sociology of texts is extremely well placed to

examine formations of this kind. To this point in time, however, textual studies most alive to the extreme variability of
the text have been grounded in hermeneutics and reading, as
we have seen. This book means to change that focus by
studying those structures of textual variability that display
themselves across a much more extensive textual field. Most
important, in our present historical situation, is to demonstrate the operation of these variables at the most material
(and apparently least "signifying" or significant) levels of the
text: in the case of scripted texts, the physical form of books
and manuscripts (paper, ink, typefaces, layouts) or their
prices, advertising mechanisms, and distribution venues. The
meanings of that most famous of middle English manuscript
collections, Harley 2253—and hence the meanings we may
imagine for the poems gathered in it—are a function of all
these matters, *whether we are aware of such matters when we
make our meanings or whether we are not.* Only in the past
ten years, however, have such materially based investigations
been rigorously pursued in relation to Harley 2253.

But the poverty of criticism in respect to such matters is
widespread, for textual studies remain largely under the spell
of romantic hermeneutics. In such a view texts, and in particular imaginative texts, are not imagined as certain kinds of
social acts; and to the degree that they *are* so imagined, the
action of the text has been too subjectively (and too ab-
stractly) conceived in its linguistic conditions.

One breaks the spell of romantic hermeneutics by socializ-
ing the study of texts at the most radical levels. This means
emphasizing two related aspects of the textual condition.
First, we must see it as an interactive locus of complex feedback operations. In the past twenty years much good work
has been done in this area. But the work has been largely confined within the material horizon of the text as that was imagined in romantic hermeneutics. A second critical move is
therefore essential. One must also demonstrate the semiotics

of the text as that has been the subject of attention of bibliographers, sociologists, economists, and tradespersons of various kinds. We must turn our attention to much more than the formal and linguistic features of poems or other imaginative fictions. We must attend to textual materials which are not regularly studied by those interested in "poetry": to typefaces, bindings, book prices, page format, and all those textual phenomena usually regarded as (at best) peripheral to "poetry" or "the text as such."

A recent study of some of these kinds of textual materials has been made by Gérard Genette in his book *Seuils*. He names his subject the set of "paratexts" that surround the central text: things like prefaces, dedications, notebooks, advertisements, footnotes, and so forth. The label "paratext" is well chosen since Genette's materials exhibit the following two characteristics: first, their textuality is exclusively linguistic; and second, they are consistently regarded as only quasi-textual, ancillary to the main textual event (i.e., to the linguistic text, or what older theorists used to call the "poem as such").[10]

The distinction, text/paratext, can be useful for certain descriptive purposes, but for a deeper investigation into the nature of textuality, it is not strong enough. For the past six years I have been exploring a different distinction by calling attention to the text as a laced network of linguistic and bibliographical codes. I continue to work from that distinction in this book. It is, for one thing, a distinction that licenses a more comprehensive study of textuality. The text/paratext distinction as formulated in *Seuils* will not, by Genette's own admission, explore such matters as ink, typeface, paper, and various other phenomena which are crucial to the understanding of textuality. They fall outside his concerns because such textual features are not linguistic. But of course all texts, like all other things human, are embodied phenomena, and the body of the text is not exclusively linguistic. By studying texts through a distinction drawn between linguistic and bibliographical codes, we gain at once a more global and a more uniform view of texts and the processes of textual production. Body is not bruised to pleasure soul.

Furthermore, and as I have already noted, the focus here is confined to works of imaginative literature (so-called) because such works foreground their materiality at the linguistic and the bibliographical levels alike. Works of belles lettres (in certain ways a better term than "literature" or "imaginative literature") can only function through what anthropologists have recently called "thick description," where excess and redundancy flourish. Were we interested here in communication theory, rather than in textuality, such redundancies would be studied as "noise," and their value for the theory would be a negative one. But the redundancy, excess, and thickness of the textual condition are positive features in the perspective I am taking. They draw our attention to that quality of self-embodiment that is so central to the nature of texts.

Of course we can treat and use texts as channels for transmitting information rather than as autopoietic mechanisms. But texts are always full of noise, and the age-old struggle with the ambiguities and paradoxes of texts registers the unhappiness of information transmitters with a medium not ideally suited to their specialized purposes.

Poets understand texts better than most information technologists. Poetical texts make a virtue of the necessity of textual noise by exploiting textual redundancy. The object of the poetical text is to thicken the medium as much as possible—literally, to put the resources of the medium on full display, to exhibit the processes of self-reflection and self-generation which texts set in motion, which they *are*.

When we imagine texts as transmitters we are not wrong in our imagination, but we *are* narrow—and much narrower than we should be if we wish to understand how texts work.

Indeed, we easily confuse investigations of textuality when we study texts as machines for carrying messages. In the reading of poetry—those paradigm texts—this kind of confusion typically arises in thematic studies, where the "meaning(s)" of the texts are pursued. In poems, however, "meaning" is mistakenly conceived if it is conceived as a "message." Rather, "meaning" in poetry is part of the poetical medium; it is a textual feature, like the work's phonetic patterns, or like its various visual components. It is one textual level— Pound called it "logopoeia"—where the text's communicative exchanges play themselves out.

One of the best ways to expose the textuality of meaning is to historicize the *logoi* we encounter in textual fields. To historicize meaning in this way is to locate it, to materialize it—to give it a local habitation and a name. Much of my critical work has been engaged in such acts of historicization. Editorial and bibliographical work, on the other hand, has been a parallel critical preoccupation because those fields do not allow one's attention to be drawn very far away from the material condition of texts. But they are fields which have for too long been frozen in positivist illusions about texts and the study of texts. It is the rare editor or bibliographer who is conscious of the semiotic function of bibliographical materials, much less of their place in the autopoietic processes of textuality as such.

This book attempts to sketch a materialist hermeneutics. In so doing, it considers texts as autopoietic mechanisms operating as self-generating feedback systems that cannot be separated from those who manipulate and use them. Their autopoiesis functions through a pair of interrelated textual embodiments we can study as systems of linguistic and bibliographical codings.

My investigations, however, are at all points located in specific textual cases. It seems to me that the extreme particularity which has been a special feature of recent "literary criticism" is a sign that texts are best approached intimately, and with special care for what makes them appear to us sui generis. Such intimacy has in the past two hundred years been commonly sought through interpretations of particular texts by particular readers.

It has been a fruitful method of study, but it has had, as well, certain evil consequences. One of these has been the privilege assigned to "meaning" in the play of the text and the consequent overemphasis upon textuality's linguistic faces. Oddly enough, the same period saw—in the actual practice of generating autopoietic texts, in the work of the writers themselves—a tremendous leap in consciousness of the semiotic potential of the text's bibliographical codes. In England this consciousness erupted most dramatically in the work of William Blake, but it can be seen throughout the period in every sort of text and not merely in those which exploit ornamental materials.

These considerations explain why this book has not set out to offer a "theory of textuality." In a sense, the only reasonable theory it might propose would have to be a kind of anti-theory, a "theory" which would refuse to attempt either a definition or even a comprehensive description of the essential features of text. What is textually possible cannot be theoretically established. What can be done is to sketch, through close and highly particular case studies, the general framework within which textuality is constrained to exhibit its transformations.

So this book is a study, not a theory, of textuality; or a set of related studies. It maps its particular investigations along the double helix of a work's reception history and its production history. But the work of knowing demands that the map be followed into the textual field, where "the meaning of the texts" will appear as a set of concrete and always changing conditions: because the meaning is in the use, and textuality is a social condition of various times, places, and persons.

PART ONE

The Garden of Forking Paths

In the fifth chamber were unnamed forms, which
cast the metals into the expanse.

There they were received by men who occupied the
sixth chamber, and took the form of books and were
arranged in libraries.

—William Blake, *The Marriage of
Heaven and Hell*

1

Theory, Literary Pragmatics, and the Editorial Horizon

AT A PANEL discussion during the 1989 meetings of the Society for Textual Scholarship (STS) I was asked the following question: "If you were editing Byron's poetry now, what would you do?"

That pragmatic (and deceptively simple) question raised complex problems in literary theory, critical method, and—finally—textual hermenuetics. It did so, however, in a particular context which now calls for some explanation. Before taking up those larger matters, therefore, I shall have to rehearse the context of the question.

When I began editing Byron in 1971 I had no special editorial expertise. I had not sought the job, was surprised when I was asked, and I accepted without knowing what would be involved in such a task. This state of original innocence is important to realize because it forced me to set aside two years for studying textual and editorial theory and method. That course of study, moreover, was undertaken from a distinctly Anglo-American perspective, which effectively meant that I kept seeing my subject within the horizon of what has come to be called the Greg-Bowers (or "eclectic") theory of editing.

Armed by these studies, I began the project of the edition: searching out the documentary materials for the texts and preparing these materials for Byron's early works (i.e., the poems written through 1815). Serious problems began to emerge very quickly, for I had decided that I would test my methodology by editing *The Giaour* first. This seemed a good thing to do because *The Giaour* involved such a large and complex body of documentary materials. As it turned out, work on *The Giaour* threw the entire project into a condition of crisis. It became clear to me that my framework of editorial theory—in effect, the theory of the eclectic edition—was not adequate to the problems presented by *The Giaour*. As I sought to solve these problems, I began a new series of investigations into textual and editorial theory—this was from 1976 to 1978. These inquiries concentrated on a historical investigation of textual studies in general, with a particular concentration on classical, biblical, and medieval textual studies from the late eighteeenth century to the present. My object was to try to understand the larger context in which the eclectic theory of editing had developed.

As a consequence, I finally began to understand what I was doing in my edition—what was possible to do, what was not possible, and why these possibilities and impossibilities existed. As the edition went forward, I no longer struggled against the limitations imposed by the Oxford English Texts series format, and I accepted that, for better and for worse, I had (undeliberately) undertaken to do a *certain kind of edition*, a critical edition squarely in the Greg-Bowers line of eclectic editing. I also accepted the fact, though far less easily, that in 1977 I was too far gone in the edition to take full advantage of computerized word processing as an editing tool. Once again my ignorance had closed down certain possibilities; and when I later (1984) learned about hypertexts and their powers, I had to swallow further regrets arising from my backward history.

What does it mean to say that an edition of Byron begun in 1987 would look very different from the one I began in 1971? Obviously it is to say that during those seventeen years I acquired a certain critical and theoretical understanding of texts and textual studies. But it is also to say that the practical and material demands of editing cut back across my previous views about theory and critical reflection in general.

Between 1971 and 1987 one overriding fact grew upon me as I worked to produce the edition of Byron: that texts are produced and reproduced under specific social and institutional conditions, and hence that every text, including those that may appear to be purely private, is a social text. This view entails a corollary understanding, that a "text" is not a "material thing" but a material event or set of events, a point in time (or a moment in space) where certain communicative interchanges are being practiced. This view of the matter—this *theoria* or way of seeing—holds true as much for the texts we inherit and study as it does for the texts we will execute ourselves.

When texts are interpreted, the readings frequently ("characteristically" is the word we should use for the period between 1940 and 1980) avoid reflecting on the material conditions of the works being "read" and the readings being executed. Those material and institutional conditions, however, are impossible to set aside if one is editing a text; and if one intends to execute a scholarly edition of a work, the social conditions of textual production become manifest and even imperative. Consequently, one comes to see that texts always stand within an editorial horizon (the horizon of their production and reproduction).

That editorial horizon entails serious consequences for the practice of literary theory *as such*—a practice (or set of practices) which came to dominate literary studies through the 1970s. Briefly, the editorial horizon forces one to reimagine the theory of texts—and, ultimately, the theory of literature—as a specific set of social operations. To the extent that recent theoretical work in literary studies has left its social dimensions unexplicated, a reasonable "resistance to theory" will be raised.[1]

But as the editorial horizon forces one to confront literary studies as a specific set of social and institutional practices, the reemergence of a sociohistorically oriented "literary pragmatics" (as it has come to be called) turns back upon editorial and bibliographical studies.[2] In twentieth-century Anglo-American studies (culminating in the scholarship of Fredson Bowers), work in these areas had become as technical, specialized, and ahistorical as the formal and thematic hermeneutics that cut a parallel course in interpretive studies.

The editorial horizon—*in the context of the 1970s and 1980s*[3]—thus came to turn back on itself and on textual studies in general by its passage through a critical encounter with literary theory. The consequence was paradoxical in the extreme, for modern textual studies—which was founded two centuries ago in the deepest kind of sociohistorical self-consciousness—now appeared to itself as a scene of narrow empiricist and even positivist practices, with habits of reflexiveness maintained merely at the technical level, as specialized goals. The sudden and even catastrophic revolution in Shakespearean textual studies in the 1970s and 1980s was both the sign and the consequence of what had been happening (and not happening) in textual studies for the previous sixty years.[4]

In this context, textual studies today have begun to move in many new directions. The editorial horizon can now be seen not merely as the locus of certain established technical procedures, but as the very emblem of what is meant by the praxis of literature and the imperative to praxis. If, therefore, one tries to acquire a comprehensive understanding of literature and textual studies—a theory of texts—one is forced in the direction of literary pragmatics. "Theory of texts" comprehends, comprises a set of practices that will be elaborated in specific social and institutional settings.

For the remainder of this discussion I want to concentrate on the idea that the theory of texts is ultimately a set of institutional (textual) practices. To elaborate the idea I will offer three case histories. Two of these represent operations I have been actively involved with, and the third—which I shall consider first—is a hypothetical case.

II

The hypothetical case involves a question very like the one I began with: If one were to edit Dante Gabriel Rossetti today, what would one do?

In a moment I will plunge into a body of detailed and even technical matters, but before doing so I must call attention to the fact that the initiating question conceals a number of other important problems and questions. For example, why ask this question of D. G. Rossetti at all, a poet who is seen by the academy as a marginal figure? One might respond by saying that Rossetti's works have not been edited since his brother William Michael undertook that task immediately after Rossetti's death over one hundred years ago.[5] This would be a perfectly good response, especially—as we shall see—in light of what we now know about the state of Rossetti's texts.

But of course the same response could be given for William Morris's poetry, or Swinburne's, or any number of other writers. Why choose Rossetti in particular—or, perhaps even more to the point, why did *I* choose Rossetti?

That form of the question is pertinent because it forces into view the ethical and cultural interests that are at stake in a proposal to edit Rossetti. The fact that Rossetti's work has been neglected is obviously relevant, but more relevant would be an explanation of Rossetti's immediate cultural importance. Why do (I think) we need Rossetti now?[6]

Furthermore, the question asks "what would one *do*," as if the editorial procedure were open to various options. This is in fact the case. Minimally one might ask whether a critical edition is being proposed, and whether the edition is being imagined as a complete edition or a selection—and why. The pursuit of these questions underlying the initial question would eventually force detailed explanations of such matters. In my particular case, it would (or should) reveal that an edition of D. G. Rossetti looms in my mind as important for two related reasons. The first I shall not deal with here: that Rossetti's work (and the world which it both reflects and interrogates) has much to say to people in (or in the orbit of) an imperial culture like that of late twentieth-century America. Second, Rossetti's works present an editor with a great opportunity: to make an edition of his writings a vehicle for displaying a significant range of issues and problems in textual criticism.

An edition of Rossetti, in short, can be imagined and carried out as a theoretical act of special importance at this critical moment in the history of textual studies. To reflect upon the possibility of such an edition is to see that making an edition—this edition in particular—is not a preinterpretive operation. By the same token, reading Rossetti (or any other author) in a particular editorial format means that one has already been set within a definite hermeneutical horizon.

In taking up the problem of editing Rossetti I will concentrate on his most important work, *The House of Life* (HL). But I must first consider briefly some of the more general problems to which I have been alluding.

Should the edition be a *Complete Works*, poetry and prose alike; or should it be *Complete Poetical Works*, perhaps with a selection of the prose? Should either of these include the translations, which represent such an extensive body of material? These are important questions, obviously, for it would make quite a difference if, for example, a press were to issue today a *Complete Works of Dante Gabriel Rossetti* rather than some sort of selection. Were I free to make a decision about such a matter, I would without question say that a *Complete Works* was needed—not merely for technical and textual reasons (e.g., the standard available editions are inadequate textually) but for larger cultural reasons as well.

But the fact is that I would not be able to make such a decision on my own—any publisher would demand a voice in the matter. This brings up another important issue: who would publish such an edition? The options here are seriously limited, for various reasons. Furthermore, given the special problems of Rossetti's texts and my theoretical goals, the choice of Oxford University Press (which would otherwise be a natural one)[7] might in the end prove too problematic.

But let us pass beyond that initial set of problems and suppose them solved in one way or another; let us suppose as well that the next practical problem, how to gather the necessary materials, has also been solved.[8] We then face the question of how to present the material that *is* to be included, and in particular how to present the work known as *The House of Life*. To answer that question we have to confront a prior question: What *is The House of Life*?[9]

It seems an easy enough question, at least if we judge by the texts that have come down to us as the standard ones used either by scholars in their specialized work, or by teachers in the classroom. But the question is no more transparent than is that master question of which it is merely a special case: "What is a text?"[10]

According to the standard classroom texts of Rossetti (e.g., Baum's, Lang's, and the texts presented in anthologies of Victorian poetry, and so forth),[11] *HL* is a sonnet sequence of 103 units—a basic group of 101 sonnets, so numbered; an introductory sonnet called "The Sonnet"; and the notorious sonnet known as 6a (originally titled "Nuptial Sleep") that was published in the 1870 version of the work by Rossetti but was subsequently withdrawn by Rossetti when he was preparing the 1881 edition of his *Poems*, where he published a 102-sonnet version of *HL*. Rossetti died in 1886 without reprinting the sonnet.

In that year his brother William Michael published his two-volume edition of his brother's *Works*, but sonnet 6a was not part of the *HL* sequence. This edition went through several reprintings, but William Michael Rossetti kept 6a out of the work until 1904, when he reinserted it. In 1911 he augmented his edition of his brother's works and explained why he kept the sonnet back in his 1886 edition, and why he finally put it back in 1904:

> My own comment on this sonnet, in the original preface to the "Collected Works" from which I omitted it, ran as follows: "'Nuptial Sleep' appeared in the volume of 'Poems' 1870 but was objected to by Mr. Buchanan, and I suppose by some other censors, as being indelicate; and my brother excluded it from 'The House of Life' in his third volume [i.e., 1881]. I consider that there is nothing in the sonnet which need imperatively banish it from his Collected Works. But his own decision commands mine: and besides it could not now be reintroduced into 'The House of Life,' which he moulded into a complete whole without it, and would be misplaced if isolated by itself—a point as to which his opinion is very plainly set forth in his prose paper, 'The Stealthy School of Criticism.'"
> As I now hold that "Nuptial Sleep" ought to be "banished" no longer, I have inserted the item in its original sequence; I number it *6a*, leaving the numeration otherwise unaltered. (653)

Although William Michael raises two strong arguments against printing sonnet 6a, when he tells us that he has changed his mind about the sonnet, he does not address either of those arguments. He simply replaces it, as if the arguments he had originally given carried no weight at all and did not have to be addressed.

No one now would print *HL* without 6a, I think, though it is important to see that in thus printing the sonnet editors are not following "the author's (final) intentions." They *are* "establishing the/a text" of *HL*, but the editorial work is completely involved in a hermeneutical operation. This is, I hasten to add, not unusual—indeed, it is what all editors do. The illusion is the idea that editors "establish" the texts that critics then go on to "interpret." All editing is an act of interpretation, and this instance from Rossetti is merely a dramatic illustration of that fact.

The appearance of 6a in 1904 was not, however, the first time the banished sonnet was printed with *HL* after Dante Gabriel Rossetti's death. It already had one posthumous appearance, in 1894, when a pirated edition of *HL* was issued by the Boston publishers Copeland and Day. In fact, this 1894 piracy has not only the full 103 sonnet sequence of *HL*, it also prints as part of the work called *The House of Life* eleven additional songs. Copeland and Day announce this as the *HL* "now for the first time given in its full text"—which text includes the eleven songs plus sonnet 6a.[12]

And the situation is still more complex. For the 1870 text printed by Rossetti—while it had those eleven songs—was a sonnet sequence of only fifty (rather than 102 or 103) sonnets. It was titled "Sonnets and Songs Toward a Work to be called 'The House of Life'." That is an important title because it shows that Rossetti (at any rate) regarded his work in 1870 as a project, or a poem in process. It is a title that might well lead one to decide—as William Michael Rossetti temporarily decided in 1886—that the 1881 text is the final one, since that text was titled, simply and with apparent conclusiveness, *The House of Life*.

The 1870 text itself was preceded by a whole series of other, earlier printed texts—most immediately, by the series of so-called trial books Rossetti had privately printed in 1869–70 which he used as working manuscripts or working proofs through which he could test out different possible versions of his work. Before that (in March 1869) he printed in

The Fortnightly Review a sequence of sixteen sonnets under the title "Of Love, Life and Death." All sixteen would eventually find a place in the work we know as *HL*. Finally, individual sonnets and sonnet groups that eventually found their way into *HL* had been printed and published at various times and places before 1870.[13]

Each of these versions mentioned so far are printed texts, though of course each traces itself back to different manuscripts. Let me summarize the situation briefly (I here leave aside the matter of sonnets published separately and not as part of an imagination of the *HL* project):

—March 1869: 16 sonnets published in *The Fortnightly Review*

—spring 1870: 50 sonnets plus 11 songs

—1881: 102 sonnets

—1894: 103 sonnets plus 11 songs

—1904 (and thereafter): 103 sonnets

This is a complex situation, but there are two other texts of the *HL* sequence (one is a distinct version; the other is not) that are important. The first of these seems relatively inconsequential except to bibliographers: I mean the 1873 Tauchnitz edition of Rossetti's works produced for a European audience. This book reproduces, with minor local alterations, the work which Rossetti had already printed at various times in England. In this edition *HL* is the 1870 version and includes sonnet 6a.

The other text is more startling and clearly alters the whole textual situation drastically. In the summer of 1871 Rossetti copied out a version of *HL* that comprised twenty-five sonnets plus five songs. None of these songs or sonnets were included in the 1869–70 printings because, in fact, they had all been written after the publication of the 1870 *Poems*, and most had been written that summer of 1871, when Rossetti was living at Kelmscott with Jane Morris. William was away at the time on a trip to Iceland. This 1871 manuscript version of *HL* is a text of *HL* that Rossetti presented to Jane Morris sometime in the late 1870s—a series of sonnets which dramatizes love as a cycle of satisfactions.[14] All of the other versions are more or less dominated by nightmare visions.

Two other matters are perhaps relevant to note here. About twenty percent of this material was written before Rossetti had any notion of the project that would come to be called *The House of Life*. In 1869 he reached back, sometimes as much as fourteen years, to choose work that had originally been written in entirely different contexts; and he would continue to do this throughout the 1870s. As for sonnet 6a, Rossetti removed this as a consequence of the attack made upon his work, and upon this sonnet in particular, by Robert Buchanan in his 1871 essay "The Fleshly School of Poetry" (published under the pseudonymn Thomas Maitland).

The question therefore is: If one were to edit this material, how would it be presented? There are, I think, three basic choices that could be made if one were imagining a book-formatted critical edition.

One could try to analyze the material in order to arrive at an ideal version—an eclectic text that would work from a basic copy-text into which would be incorporated certain materials from texts other than the copy-text. Classically, this might work by choosing the 1881 text as copy-text (or perhaps the ultimate corrected proofs for 1881) and, through a process of collation, introduce into 1881 any changes deemed necessary—for example, most dramatically, sonnet 6a. Basically, this is what was done by William Michael Rossetti in 1904 and 1911, and later by Baum and Lang, so that this is the text most readers now work from.

Second, one could distinguish a series of versions and offer diplomatic texts of each one, adding (perhaps) a set of collations where necessary. This would yield at least four distinct *House[s] of Life*:

—the 16-sonnet version of 1869
—the 50-sonnet and 11-song version of 1870
—the 25-sonnet and 5-song version of 1871
—the 102-sonnet version of 1881

In this case sonnet 6a would not belong in any version but the one that appeared in 1870. Collations would be complex only for the 1870 and the 1881 texts.

One might also present a fifth version, that is, the 103-sonnet version constructed for Rossetti's work after his death by his brother and subsequent editors. In this version some accommodation would have to be made for the various "songs," which might be included in an appendix.

The third option is to treat the entire corpus of material as an evolving compositional or historical project and attempt to construct a text which would represent that textual evolution. This would produce one of two kinds of evolutionary texts. One would be a "genetic text," in the manner of various editions currently being pursued in Europe—in which case the text would ignore the published texts (and perhaps the trial books as well) and strive to produce a continuous compositional text—a portrait of the authorial process of creation.

A modified version of this procedure can be observed, for example, in Hans Gabler's edition of *Ulysses*. That model's variations from the usual "genetic" edition point toward the second type of evolutionary text one might try to produce: not a "continuous manuscript text" (as Gabler has called it) but a "continuous production text," where the effort is to display the work's evolution from its earliest to its latest productive phases in the author's lifetime. This last procedure would be difficult to manage, however, because Rossetti's *HL* evolved radially even as it was also evolving "continuously." One sees this radial development most clearly in the way Rossetti temporarily decides to include, or to remove, the sequence of associated songs; one sees it as well in the twenty-five sonnet five-song version that he gave to Jane Morris (a clear radial version); and one sees it finally in the existence of the 1873 Tauchnitz edition of Rossetti's works. This edition was produced under Rossetti's supervision, and it includes the 1870 version of *HL*.

I must pause to consider the 1873 Tauchnitz edition a bit further. In one sense the edition is clearly a radial development of Rossetti's work in *HL*, and, thus, is kin to the Jane Morris manuscript text and to the texts that play with the inclusion of the song material. The Tauchnitz edition is a variant of the 1870 version in which sonnet 6a does not figure as a problematical passage because the Tauchnitz edition is produced for a different—that is to say, for a non-English—audience. Furthermore, this 1873 edition shows that Rossetti regarded 1870 as a relatively integral work, something that could be reprinted with only minor local changes in the text. In fact, the 1870 edition was reprinted five times up to 1872. The 1881 edition evolves from the 1870 text, and even supersedes it in a sense; but 1881 does not obliterate the integrity of the 1870 edition, any more than it does the integrity of the other versions of the work.

In this situation, were I editing *HL* I would certainly choose either the second option or the continuous production text of the third option. But that practical editorial matter is not my principal concern at this moment. Rather, I am concerned with clarifying how each of the editorial options impinges on the interpretation of the work.

This can be done by invoking the distinctions comprehended by the terms, "text," "poem," and "work." Each term frames the literary product in a different way. The "text" is the literary product conceived as a purely lexical event; the "poem" is the locus of a specific process of production (or reproduction) and consumption; and the "work" comprehends the global set of all the texts and poems which have emerged in the literary production and reproduction processes.[15] Looking at Rossetti's *HL* in these terms we can see how a choice of editorial procedure will amount to a profound hermeneutic definition of Rossetti's work.

If one edited along the lines of the first option, for example, one would be foregrounding *HL* as a "poem" and as a "text"—as well as privileging one particular version of *HL* as "poem." This interpretive emphasis would follow from the editor's desire to pursue *HL* as a single authoritative production. If one were to choose the second option, one would be foregrounding the "poem" and the "work," because such an edition presents *HL* to us in a series of discrete versions that are related to each other through discontinuous (and not exclusively authorial) filiations. If one chose option three, one would privilege the "text" and the "work" because a major part of the production process is foregrounded in the editorial process. One could also say that the third option would frame Rossetti's materials for stylistic, intertextual, and sociohistorical readings. Option two, on the other hand, would set *HL* for structural, formal, and sociohistorical inquiries. The first option—which is the option that dominated editing during the period of New Critical hermeneutics—organizes the material along lines that call out stylistic and formal investigations.

Let us suppose that I chose the second option—that is, that I chose to edit so that four, or perhaps five, different versions were presented as independent units. To do this immediately sets a privilege upon *HL* as a set of integral poetic units, each of which could be "read" on its own in the manner of any New Critical, structural, or even deconstructive reading (for all are formalistically grounded operations). But because each of the versions would stand in the edition in a set of differential relations with the others, the reader would also be urged to investigate those sets of relations. Many sorts of reading could be generated from such a situation, but it is certain that sociohistorical factors would enter into the investigations—for the simple reason that the edition has brought strongly to our attention issues of textual production, as well as other social and contextual matters that bear upon the very existence of multiple versions.

So we conclude that producing editions is one of the ways we produce literary meanings; and, we see once again that this aspect of literary production is as complex as all the others and involves a ramified set of interconnected individuals and institutions. We are reminded, finally, that every part of the productive process is meaning-constitutive—so that we are compelled, if we want to understand a literary work, to examine it in all its multiple aspects. The words that lie immediately before a reader on some page provide one with the merest glimpse of that complex world we call literary work and the meanings it produces. We all start from some localized place of reading, but no one who reads seriously will ever end up there—or if you do return, you will see that place very differently, perhaps begin to see it truly only then for the first time.

I I I

Consider the following story, which is not a hypothetical case but a brief narrative of my involvement in a current editorial project.

Several years ago Oxford University Press asked me to edit *The New Oxford Book of Romantic Poetry*. I thought about it briefly and declined. Shortly afterwards Roger Lonsdale published his splendid *New Oxford Book of Eighteenth-Century Verse*. This work had so completely reimagined the Oxford anthology along historicist lines that it made me see what might be done for the poetry of the romantic period. I therefore reversed my original decision about doing the edition.

To edit such an anthology is to set forth a constellation of related (and relative) literary judgments in historical terms. Even to decide on the chronological limits of a "romantic" anthology is to pass certain judgments. In the present case the "romantic" anthology will comprise the years 1785 to 1832, for reasons that I shall indicate shortly.

The problem of chronology is, in this case, only a special aspect of a more general problem that students of the romantic period often lose sight of: that the poetry of the period is by no means monologically "romantic." This truth even appears in the historiography of the previous *Oxford Book of Romantic Verse* edited by H. S. Milford. When this anthology was first published in 1928, Milford titled it the *The Oxford Book of Regency Verse*. It was given its new title when it went into a second printing, in 1935.[16]

The discrepancy between the words "romantic" and "regency" calls attention to far more than a chronological differential. It reminds us that the poetry of the period need not be imagined only in terms of the work of the six so-called great romantics. Other frames of reference were once operative, and remain significant. It makes a great difference, for example, if one takes Burns's *Poems, Chiefly in the Scottish Dialect* (1786) as a point of departure for the period rather than Blake's *Songs* (1789–93) or Wordsworth's and Coleridge's *Lyrical Ballads* (1798).[17]

The work of Burns calls attention to a pair of related but perhaps even more serious problems in our literary and cultural histories. The first of these concerns the years 1790 to 1800, a period of great literary significance and even greater literary volatility. Our poetry anthologies give little sense of the kind of writing that dominated this important cultural scene. To take only one problem: romantic ideology, which privileges conventions of "sincerity" over conventions of

"premeditation," has all but obliterated our received sense of
the satiric traditions that were being worked between 1790
and 1832. The satiric tradition in the years 1790 to 1832 is
strong and continuous, and includes people like William
Hone, Moore, James and Horace Smith, John Hookham
Frere, Winthrop Mackworth Praed, Peacock, Hood, and William Frederick Deacon. In this context the period of the
1790s is especially important because it is the period when
those traditions were being laid down, most significantly in
the poetical wars that raged over issues connected with the
French Revolution.

Of course we remember—if we remember at all—the brilliant reactionary satire of *The Poetry of the Anti-Jacobin*. But
do we remember that the precursors of that work were William Gifford's *The Baviad* (1791) and *The Maeviad* (1795)?
I recall them here, however, not because they are especially
interesting as poetry. His two satires, "famous in [their]
time," are scholastic machines turning out pure products of
pedantic wit (if that phrase be not a contradiction in itself).
The Baviad and *The Maeviad* ought to be holding our attention today not on their own behalf, but on behalf of their satiric objects: I mean the (at that time notorious) school of
writers known as the Della Cruscans.

The Della Cruscans did not write satire—on the contrary,
they wrote sentimental and erotic poetry. More, they
achieved great celebrity and influence by transforming the
public pages of various magazines, like *The European Magazine*, *The World*, and *The Oracle*, into a kind of love-theatre
of poetry where (for example) Robert Merry, writing as
"Della Crusca," would engage in poetic love dialogues with
(for example) Mrs. Anna Cowley (writing as "Anna Ma-
tilda"). The romantic love poetry of Byron, Shelley, and
Keats constitutes a massive act of invisible appropriation of
the erotic tradition these writers set in motion. As poetical
children of Laurence Sterne, the Della Cruscans and their

early imitators drove conservative figures like Gifford and J. T. Mathias to their satiric denunciations.[18] *The Poetry of the Anti-Jacobin* is part of that reactive tradition, just as Richard Polwhele's *The Unsex'd Females* (1798) is part of the reaction.

I mention the latter in this connection because it is a poem that lays out most explicitly the case of the reactionaries' grievances. To Polwhele, English poetry in the 1790s had been invaded by women who write on subjects they should not be writing about, least of all in public. The Della Cruscan movement is partly to blame for the infamous transportation of their Italian coterie verse (e.g., *The Florence Miscellany*, 1785) from Florence to London. But the evil represented by Della Cruscan poetry is greatly exacerbated by having entered England at the worst of times—just as the jacobinical ideas of the revolution were gaining interest and support.

Only in this context will one be able to appreciate the importance of the poetry of 1790s writers like Helen Maria Williams or (slightly later) Charlotte Dacre. Indeed, only in this context will one be able to understand the intimate relation that holds between those two (apparently so divergent) strains in the poetry of Thomas Moore: on one hand, his political work (supporting Irish independence, and attacking English imperialism), and on the other, his sentimental-erotic love poetry.

Or imagine an anthology that emphasized the importance of the translations of Sir William Jones. The appearance of the *Asiatic Miscellany* in 1787, which Jones coedited and which contained several of his most influential translations, was an important event in literary history as well as in anthropology. Romantic anthologies now do not recognize the impact those translations made, not merely in the development of orientalism, but as part of the new ethnological approach to literature and cultural production. It was the romantic period that set in motion a drive for translations and imitations that were imagining themselves along anthropological lines. This is very different from the approaches toward poetical translation that antedate the coming of Macpherson and Chatterton.

These examples mean to say, simply, that a reimagination of the poetry of the romantic period might well begin with a reimagination of the poetry of the 1790s in England. To reshape the poetry of the 1790s is to have begun a more comprehensive rereading of the work of the entire period that stretches into the 1830s. Such a reimagination, however, requires as well an understanding of the significance of the Della Cruscan movement, of Burns's 1786 volume, and of the orientalist writing initiated by the translations of Sir William Jones.

In that larger context, moreover, we have to confront yet another "dark age"—by which I mean the poetry that appeared between the death of Byron (1824) and the publication of Tennyson's *Poems* (December 1832). So far as poetry is concerned these are the years which literary historians have seen as standing between two worlds, one dying and the other apparently not ready to be born. Literary history has found them embarrassing years, a period dominated by "scribbling" women and their supposedly vapid literary outlets, those infamous "Annuals" like *Friendship's Offering* and *Forget Me Not* that began to appear on the scene in 1823. The Tennyson and Browning of our received histories could not come soon enough to put those years out of memory.

And it is *in fact* true that the 1820s were dominated by women's poetry, were dominated by two writers in particular: Felicia Hemans, the most published poet of the nineteenth century (more published even than Byron), and Laetitia Elizabeth Landon, a late romantic writer now all but forgotten. Landon's work (she published under the initials L.E.L.) went through numerous editions and clearly had a major impact on the writing of Tennyson in particular—

although literary history seems to have all but completely forgotten that fact. In her meteoric career she articulated, for
the first time in a comprehensive way, an English and female
version of the sorrows of Werther. Her tragic and mysterious death in 1838 became a commemorative date of enormous significance for English women poets for the rest of the
century.

It seems clear to me that we no longer know how to read
a poet like Landon, and that we have lost all connection with
the Sternian legacy inherited and transformed by the Della
Cruscans. More than that, our readings of the so-called great
romantics continue to be pursued under such historical ignorance as to blind us to much of what is happening even in that
work we seem so familiar with. Marlon Ross's recently published *The Contours of Masculine Desire* (1989) represents
an important new intervention into this situation—a reading
of the "major" romantics in the context of those networks of
desire which their poetry skirts, represses, and transforms.

The New Oxford Book of Verse of the Romantic Period
will be attempting some similar, as well as some other, re-
visionary moves through its editorial policies and procedures.
These departures are to be signaled in the title of the book
itself, which is not decided as yet, but which—in *any* case—
will not be able to follow the standard formula "of Victorian
Poetry," "of Eighteenth-Century Poetry," "of Romantic
Poetry."[19]

In general, the anthology will try to represent more comprehensive and accurate "contours" for the poetical work
being done between 1785 and 1832. The aim is to open the
field of such writing beyond the limits that have been so carefully erected during the past one hundred and fifty years.
Those limits have been defined through certain overlapping
but closely related "romantic ideologies," the two most significant of which have been those descending to us through

Wordsworth and through Byron. There are, of course, other romantic ideologies—Blake's, for example, is a late but quite a distinctive development. One of these is the line I associate with certain women writers, though Sterne is probably its immediate point of departure.

By no means did all the women who wrote between 1785 and 1832 fall into any of these romantic lines, however. Felicia Hemans, for example, plainly and directly draws upon both of those very different legacies of Wordsworth and Byron, but her own work could scarcely be more different from either of them. On the contrary, the arena of Hemans's work—the site of its preoccupations as well as its contradictions—is fundamentally domestic.

We want to remember this because it calls our attention, once again, to the fact that the period 1785 to 1832 is marked by many more differentials than the rubric "romantic poetry"—however variously that term is understood—will be able to comprehend. This new edition will try to honor those differentials. To do so asks for the display of a large population of writers, many of whom were not principally—or even "professionally"—"poets." The broadening of the poetic franchise seems to me an imperative scholarly task, particularly at this time when certain narrow and even imperial concepts of writing and culture are once again seeking to define the limits of what is best and culturally possible. The edition, in short, will be trying to reimagine the field of poetical writing from 1785 to 1832, and through that reimagination to continue a further reimagination of the later history of writing in English.

IV

The foregoing are two specific tasks that illustrate how editorial horizons establish the field in which hermeneutical questions are raised and addressed. In this respect, these examples point toward more general issues in pedagogy and the need to reintegrate textual and bibliographical studies into the literary curriculum.

That need brings me to my final subject: curricular procedures in graduate literary studies today.

The social text, the praxis of theory, and the editorial horizon of interpretation: although each of these (interrelated) ideas can and should be argued in a study like this, they require a clear and straightforward curricular methodology if they are to establish for themselves something more than a passing interest. Here is a sketch of the program I have been following, with some success, for the past ten years in my graduate seminars.[20]

The class is divided into weekly study units with two or three students responsible for each unit. While the class at large reads the week's assigned materials, the study group prepares a report on the material along with an agenda of questions and topics for discussion. The report and agenda is distributed to the students one day before the class meeting.

The rule is that the study group will provide the class with a detailed analytical description of (a) a history of the texts that are to be taken up in class, and (b) a history of the receptions of those texts. The report must include as well a bibliography of materials that are deemed essential for studying the history of the text and the history of the receptions.

Obviously neither of these two investigative lines could, under the constraints of a graduate seminar, be presented exhaustively. This limitation, however, offers as many opportunites as it does problems. Under such conditions the student has to address these tasks of sociohistorical reconstruction in very self-conscious and deliberate ways—choosing a particular focus on some part of the historical materials, and deliberately letting the rest go.

The function of these research and classroom protocols is to make students confront the textual horizon(s) of the various works they are studying. The procedures ask the student to realize, in very particular ways, how and why one must speak of texts as "social." The exercises are "elementary" in the sense that they do not by themselves put the student in touch with the most complex sociohistorical and ideological issues engaged by literary work. Nevertheless, requiring detailed reports about the production, distribution, and reception of specific texts gives a sharp focus to the larger historical and literary problems that center in the texts.

In the initial classes I assume the student's role and prepare the report, the bibliography, and the set of questions for class discussion. I make this move to supply a possible model for the students when they have to prepare their own reports and class discussion agendas. A recent course in romantic legacies, for example, began with a class on Blake's *Songs of Innocence and of Experience*. The report distributed to the class ran as follows:

I. *Textual history*

The poems in the collections were written between the mid-1780s and 1797, with the *Innocence* poems being generally earlier. Blake's early *Notebook* (so-called the Rossetti Manuscript because it was once owned by D. G. Rossetti) contains his drafts of many of the *Experience* poems, dating from about 1791–93. Four poems from *Innocence* (pls. 13, 15, 19, 24) appeared in other contexts before the first (1789) printing of the *Innocence* sequence.

The *Notebook* drafts provide some detailed information about the composition process for some of Blake's most interesting works, including "The Tyger."

Innocence was published first as a separate sequence—earliest copy, 1789. *Experience* was first published as a separate copy in 1794, or possibly 1793. The two sequences were only printed together as the combined *Songs* between 1819–1828. Before that they were sold as separate sequences, which

41

could, however, be combined together, and which in some cases were.

The order of the plates in the various sequences varies greatly, although the now traditional order of 1–54 tended to prevail in Blake's latest copies (1819–28). These late copies tend also to be the most elaborately colored and produced.

After Blake's death, a number of copies were printed from Blake's surviving copperplates, and a few were colored. These copperplates were later destroyed, so that only a small fragment of any of Blake's original copperplates for his Illuminated books survives to this day (a portion of an *America* variant plate).

Reprints and facsimiles: only two small editions (1839, 1843) were issued before the publication of Alexander Gilchrist's important *Life* (1863). After that Blake's reputation began to increase steadily and a number of editions and facsimiles began to appear.

Appended to this report are the relevant pages from Bentley's *Blake Books* where he discusses certain important aspects of the physical appearance of the texts of *Songs*.

Note: Blake's method of production (he was self-published, and the books were both expensive and difficult to produce) diminished his access to the normal institutions of reception (he was not reviewed, e.g.). The *Songs* were far and away his most "successful" work—twenty-one copies of *Innocence* descend to us, and twenty-seven copies of the combined *Songs*.

The physical constitution of these *Songs*—their sequencing in the different copies as well as their textual formatting, punctuation, and the physical appearance of the texts (including the ornamental materials)—is highly relevant to any study of their meaning.

II. *Reception history*

This can be conveniently divided into four phases:

1. 1783–1828: The period between the publication of

Blake's *Poetical Sketches* and his death. During this period Blake was known primarily as an engraver and a painter. His poetical work circulated in a small circle of friends and art connoisseurs. Although Blake is often associated with radical London circles of the 1790s, his poems did not interact within that circle in any important or observable way. After his three years' sojourn in Felpham he returned to London but spent the rest of his life almost completely removed from radical political contacts; his friends were almost exclusively pious evangelical Christians. Southey, Lamb, Coleridge, and Wordsworth all had some acquaintance with his work after his Felpham years, but only Lamb was strongly impressed, and even he was not moved to disseminate Blake's work.

2. 1828–1862: The invisible years. Blake's work in this period is preserved in the very private memories of a small group of friends and admirers, mostly young evangelicals. As readers of Blake they tended to ignore or downplay the political character of Blake's radical ideas; the emphasis was upon Blake as a Christian visionary.

3. 1863–1946: The period in which Blake's work began to be widely and favorably received. The key event is the discovery of Blake by D. G. Rossetti and his collaboration in the publication of Alexander Gilchrist's *Life of William Blake* (1863). Swinburne's study of Blake (1865) and Yeats's enthusiasm were also pivotal. In this period the previously dominant "line" of reception, which was religious, succeeds to an interest in Blake as a point of departure for the intertwined cultural interests of the aesthetic and the symbolist movements in England.

4. 1947–present: The period of Blake's academic apotheosis, which dates from the publication of Frye's *Fearful Symmetry* (1947). Here previous lines of interest are more programmatically pursued. Blake has been congenial to almost every type of professional interest, and the *Songs* in particular have become a standard source of school texts.

Bibliography
Standard (typographical) edition:

David V. Erdman, ed. *The Complete Poetry and Prose of William Blake*, newly revised ed., with commentary by Harold Bloom (Berkeley and Los Angeles, 1982). A modernized version of this text has been reprinted in R. L. Stevenson's edition of Blake's poetry produced for the Longman's series; this edition has excellent brief commentaries and notes.

Facsimiles:

The Trianon Press facsimiles of Blake's works are the best and best known, but there have been many of all the works, and especially of the *Songs*. See Bentley's *Blake Books* for details.

Bibliographical tools:

G. E. Bentley, Jr. *Blake Books* (Oxford, 1977). Indispensable guide both to Blake's own works and to all subsequent materials about him and his works, including editions, criticism, etc.

————. *Blake Records* (Oxford, 1969). Also indispensable: Collects all life notices about Blake and his family by friends, acquaintances, and contemporaries. A *Supplement* was issued in 1988.

David V. Erdman. *A Concordance to the Writings of William Blake* (Ithaca, 1967).

G. E. Bentley, Jr., ed. *William Blake's Writings*. 2 vols. (Oxford, 1978). A typographical edition with elaborate and useful bibliographical materials.

Note: General bibliographical guides to all aspects of Blake criticism can be found in *A Blake Bibliography* (1964), edited by Bentley and Martin K. Nurmi. Also important are the various MLA-issued "Guides to Research and Criticism"; see *The English Romantic Poets and Essayists* of 1957 and 1966, and *The English Romantic Poets* (Frank Jordan, ed. 1985) for three good bibliographical essays. *Blake Studies* and the *Blake Newsletter* are important resources, as are the annual MLA bibliography and the *Cambridge Bibliography of English Literature.*

Reception history:

Deborah Dorfman. *Blake in the Nineteenth Century* (1969).

G. E. Bentley, Jr., ed. *William Blake: The Critical Heritage* (1975). The introduction here is an abridged version of Bentley's essay "Blake's Reputation and Interpreters" in *Blake Books.*

Songs: Editions and Critical Materials

An important resource is William Blake's Notebook, which has been twice produced in facsimile (in 1935 by Geoffrey Keynes, and in 1973 by David V. Erdman). The academic literature on the *Songs* is now quite large: appended here are the relevant pages from Mary Lynn Johnson's bibliographical essay on Blake printed in the 1985 MLA guides to research (see above).

A number of school editions have been produced, as well as collections of critical essays; these can be found listed in *Blake Books* and in Johnson's essay.

Topics for Discussion

1. The various plates move around a great deal in the extant copies of the *Songs*. What difference do (or might) these changes make for a reader? Consider, for example, "The Voice of the Ancient Bard," which moves from *Innocence* to *Experience* (and occupies several positions in each sequence). Consider also "The School-Boy." Or "The Little Girl Found."

2. "Read" the page layout of "The Fly" and "Ah! Sunflower."

3. The lost/found motif is strong in both sequences (echoing the Christian topos, as in the hymn "Amazing Grace": "I once was lost, but now am found,/ Was blind, but now I see"). How Christian, in what way "Christian," are the *Songs*?

4. Answer the question posed in "The Tyger": "Did he

who make the Lamb make thee?" Elaborate. Or are we not supposed to answer it?

5. What can we say about the different "audiences" of the *Songs*? In general, what difference does it make that we be conscious of an audience? Of ourselves as audience, or ourselves in relation to other possible (or actual) audiences?

6. Notice the punctuation of poems like "Infant Joy," "The Dream," and (in *Experience*) "Introduction" and "Earth's Answer."

7. Are the *Songs* "lyric poems?" In what way? Is there a difference between a "lyric poem" and a "song" that can or even should be made in the case of these works (but perhaps not for other works).

This report, needless to say, does not deal with every topic that might be imagined essential for a study of the *Songs'* textuality. Notably absent is any consideration of Blake's graphic methods of production, for example. Indeed—and this is specifically explained to the class—a number of other reports might have been prepared with very different emphases. The textual part of the report might easily have been given over completely to an introduction to Blake's printmaking methods in general, with particular attention to these early *Songs*. The transmission history, on the other hand, might have chosen to limit itself to one or another period of the total history. The students should tailor the reports to their particular interests. What is essential is that they engage with literary work through highly particular studies of the production, transmission, and reception histories of specific texts.

One further course protocol for these graduate seminars should be mentioned. Besides the seminar reports (and a final critical paper, which usually turns out to be an expansion of material initially developed in one or another of the reports), the students are held responsible for a collective project. This project is specifically editorial. The class may be asked to edit a particular text (e.g., Blake's *The French Revolution*) or to produce an outline or proposal for an edition of a larger work (e.g., an edition of Wordsworth's five-book *Prelude* or of Byron's *Poems* [1816]). In these cases the editorial horizon has to be confronted within a set of perspectives that are very different from those developed in the individual class reports.

One interpretive consequence of this course requirement is to situate the students' interests in literary criticism within the orbit of the practical work of scholarship. Texts and their editions are produced for particular purposes by particular people and institutions, and they may be used (and reused) in multiple ways, many of which run counter to uses otherwise or elsewhere imagined. To edit a text is to be situated in a historical relation to the work's transmissions, but it is also to be placed in an immediate relation to contemporary cultural and conceptual goals. Nor are these simply the goals and purposes of the editor-as-technical-functionary. While that· imagination of the editorial horizon remains common among editors and hermeneuts alike, it is deeply mistaken—not a "blinded" imagination but a deluded one.[21] Carrying forward an actual editorial project, in a context where bibliography and interpretation are continually being forced to confront each other, leaves the student less room for mistaking those purposes and goals.

2

What Is Critical Editing?

UNTIL quite recently, when textual scholars in the United States occupied themselves with theoretical issues of textuality, they turned for guidance to editing and editorial theory. Many unfortunate consequences have followed from these narrowly empiricist inclinations, as I have argued elsewhere.[1] Because of the great influence which American scholarship exerted upon Western philology since World War II, this empiricism has caused greatest damage to our philosophical understanding of textuality in general.

The problem appears with special clarity if we pose the question, "What is critical editing?" This is a technical question within the arena of editorial studies, because terms like "critical editing" and "critical edition" have acquired, during the past forty years, a new and highly specialized meaning. That new meaning can be traced through all American and most English work in editorial theory of the period.

A convenient summary of this line of thought will be found in the Modern Language Association's recent (1985) handbook *An Introduction to Bibliographical and Textual Studies*.[2] The handbook distinguishes three types of editing: documentary editing, critical editing, and historical-critical editing. The first is clear enough, the last is a bow in the direction of Hans Zeller and the recent European tradition of "genetic" editing, and the middle term signifies no less (and

48

no more) than the idea of "eclectic" editing as established by an editorial tradition associated with the name of Fredson Bowers.[3] According to this tradition,

> Critical editing . . . does not reproduce the text of a particular document but produces an eclectic text based on several texts and on editorial emendations. It assumes that though multiple texts of a work may vary in authority, no one text is entirely authoritative. (Williams and Abbott, 56)

And furthermore:

> A critically edited text, when combined with an apparatus that presents the evidence used in the text's construction and that lists the variants of the authoritative states, is called a "critical edition." (Williams and Abbott, 57)

So far these ideas about critical editing differ little from the thinking of F. A. Wolf or Karl Lachmann or August Boeckh, three foundational theorists in the tradition of German Enlightenment philology. The difference appears, however, at the next step of the presentation, when "some basis on which to judge the authority of the variant readings" is sought.

At this point we learn that "in critical editing . . . authorial intention is the dominant authority." Consequently:

> The method of critical editing, then, is (1) to discover the variant readings of a text and to adopt those that represent the author's final intention and (2) to detect erroneous (i.e., nonauthorial) readings and to correct them by proposing readings that more accurately represent what the author intended to write. To accomplish this, an editor selects a "copy-text"—the one state of the text that is determined to be most authoritative—and then emends it. (Williams and Abbott, 58)

Here two concepts are particularly crucial. This imagination of "critical editing" pushes the specialized issue of copy-text to the fore, along with the (not necessarily) related issue of author's intentions. Furthermore, the theory assumes that the "critical issues" are linguistic issues.

In a more comprehensive imagination of the fields of textual criticism and critical editing, however, the term "critical" refers to nothing more than the comparative analysis of multiple texts. This view sees textual criticism born of the awareness that texts descend to us through a more or less complex, more or less fractured, transmission history. The business of textual criticism—and hence of critical editing and the critical edition—is in this view twofold: to expose the entire network of transmissive variation in an analytic (as opposed to a purely positivistic) way; and to define and set aside those transmissive variations which can be shown to be corruptions. Neither of these goals entails, as a necessity, the production of an "eclectic" text.

When one begins to prepare a scholarly edition, it makes a great difference which idea of critical editing one subscribes to: (a) the production of an eclectic text, or (b) the production of an edition which displays and analyzes the historical descent of the work.

For example, suppose one were to undertake a critical edition of Matthew Arnold's poetry. In this case every critical editor would begin with the same general object of (a) assembling a complete history of the texts as they descend to us, and (b) analyzing the lines of transmission of these texts. When the textual collations had been completed, each editor would discover approximately the same situation with respect to the verbal text: that the texts do not vary greatly, and that the factor of textual corruption is quite low.

The status of a particularly important work like *Empedocles on Etna* is typical. One need only peruse Kenneth Allott's recent critical edition of Arnold's poetry to see that the text of this poem has remained relatively error-free.[4] From that situation one might also come to believe that the text is a highly stable text, and hence that one edition of the poem—say Arnold's first edition, printed in 1852—does not vary much from the second edition, printed in 1867. Indeed, the linguistic variations between these two texts are minimal.

In fact, however, the *Empedocles* of 1852 and the *Empedocles* of 1867, though linguistically congruent, represent radically different texts. It seems to me the business of critical editing to make those differences clear.[5]

The first scholarly editor of Arnold's poems, H. S. Milford, understood the situation very well and made an excellent move in trying to deal with it. What he did appears most dramatically in his table of contents, which includes a list of the separate tables of contents of all of Arnold's poems as they appeared in the different volumes (and magazines) up to 1867.[6] *Empedocles* is therefore listed under that name twice in this table of contents, though its text is printed only once.

Milford's table of contents, on closer examination, displays the dance of Arnold's poems as they appeared or disappeared or changed their positions in the various editions he brought out through 1867. These bibliographical—as opposed to linguistic—variations are of the greatest importance for anyone wishing to understand Arnold's poetry.

Milford's table of contents, a shrewd critical move, of course only schematizes a set of critical investigations which could have been, and probably should have been, carried out far more thoroughly. But I am not concerned here with the specific shortcomings of Milford's edition. What interests me is how Milford's edition is imagining the idea of the "critical edition." Though he is working with a modern and not an ancient text, Milford's mind has far more in common with minds like Wolf's, or Lachmann's, or Boeckh's, or A. E. Housman's than it does with post–World War II American eclectic editors. More to the point, his edition has reaped great benefits from what might otherwise be taken as its historical backwardness.

In *Empedocles on Etna*, for example, Milford had to contend with a text which was at once highly unstable and, at the same time, relatively error-free. This kind of text is extremely common, especially in the modern periods. Among the poets, Dante Gabriel Rossetti provides an outstanding, even a labyrinthine, example of the same thing, as does Walter Savage Landor. The novelistic examples are even more apparent and ready to hand.

The multiple texts of *Empedocles on Etna* or *The House of Life* do not lend themselves to a textual analysis which focusses issues of textual variance only at the linguistic level. Linguistic variation in *The House of Life* is, unlike *Empedocles*, very high, but it is variation which eclectic editing cannot come to grips with. So-called facing-page editions, like DeSelincourt's famous treatment of *The Prelude*, or Gabler's recent edition of *Ulysses*, may or may not illuminate the critical issues. That question can only be decided by testing how well the edition has critically elucidated the full play of the work's bibliographical (as opposed to its linguistic) codes.

This distinction, between a work's bibliographical and its linguistic codes, is fundamentally important for textual criticism, and hence for critical editing. Without making and implementing the distinction in detailed ways, textual critics cannot fully elucidate—cannot analyze—the lines of materials which descend to them.

Let me begin to illustrate what I mean with another example—a distinguished piece of work by one of the most distinguished living editors of texts of the romantic period, David V. Erdman: *The Complete Poetry and Prose of William Blake*.[7] This is a critical edition which has gone through one major editorial revision, and which has been awarded the Modern Language Association's editorial seal of distinction. It is the standard current edition of Blake.

Now look at the two reproductions of the first text page of Blake's consummate work *Jerusalem* (one depicting the text as Blake originally produced it, and the same text in Erdman's critical edition)[8] (see illus. 1 and 2). The illustrations tell what ought to be a familiar story, though editors and textual theorists continue to neglect or obfuscate the point: that editing, including critical editing, is more an act of translation than of reproduction. When we edit we change, and even good editing, like Erdman's, necessarily involves fundamental departures from "authorial intention," however that term is interpreted.

The last point needs to be underlined. Erdman gives us a text that hardly corresponds to what Blake intended or might have intended at any time. We all see that a fundamental difference stands between an illuminated and a typographical text. But that graphic and unmistakable difference merely foregrounds the general character of the situation. The Blake text is iconic, for example, whereas the Erdman text is radically dispersed through the book as a reading text, an apparatus criticus, and textual notes, as well as various other materials. All critical editions carry out such acts of dispersal, and to that extent they reflect certain "intentions" of the author in the present (Erdman) rather than the author in the past (Blake).

In one sense the Erdman edition is a travesty of Blake's original authorial intentions—and indeed, there are Blakists who refuse to teach Blake out of the Erdman text, who insist upon facsimile editions as a minimal point of departure for study. But if Erdman's edition is a travesty in one sense, why has it been awarded the Modern Language Association's seal of editorial excellence? Is Erdman's a good edition? The answer is clearly "yes." Erdman is a scrupulous and accurate editor, and his edition has managed to translate Blake's illuminated work into a reasonable set of typographical equivalences. Besides, its apparatus criticus is comprehensive and quite meticulous.

Nevertheless, the edition has serious problems precisely because it is a typographical translation.[9] Most important, perhaps, is the fact that the typographical format has forced

1. William Blake, *Jerusalem* plate 3 (from Trianon Press
facsimile edition of the Cunliffe copy, reproduced in monochrome).

SHEEP   GOATS

To the Public

After my three years slumber on the banks of the Ocean, I again display my Giant forms to the Public: My former Giants & Fairies having reciev'd the highest reward possible: the [love] and [friendship] of those with whom to be connected, is to be [blessed]: I cannot doubt that this more consolidated & extended Work, will be as kindly recieved

The Enthusiasm of the following Poem, the Author hopes [no Reader will think presumptuousness or arroganc[e] when he is reminded that the Ancients acknowledge their love to their Deities, to the full as Enthusiastically as I have who Acknowledge mine for my Saviour and Lord, for they were wholly absorb'd in their Gods.] I also hope the Reader will be with me, wholly One in Jesus our Lord, who is the God [of Fire] and Lord [of Love] to whom the Ancients look'd and saw his day afar off, with trembling & amazement.

The Spirit of Jesus is continual forgiveness of Sin: he who waits to be righteous before he enters into the Saviours kingdom, the Divine Body; will never enter there. I am perhaps the most sinful of men! I pretend not to holiness! yet I pretend to love, to see, to converse with daily, as man with man, & the more to have an interest in the Friend of Sinners. Therefore [Dear] Reader, [forgive] what you do not approve, & [love] me for this energetic exertion of my talent.

> Reader! [lover] of books! [lover] of heaven,
> And of that God from whom [all books are given,]
> Who in mysterious Sinais awful cave
> To Man the wond'rous art of writing gave,
> Again he speaks in thunder and in fire!   5
> Thunder of Thought, & flames of fierce desire:
> Even from the depths of Hell his voice I hear,
> Within the unfathomd caverns of my Ear.
> Therefore I print; nor vain my types shall be:
> Heaven, Earth & Hell, henceforth shall live in harmony   10

Of the Measure, in which
the following Poem is written

We who dwell on Earth can do nothing of ourselves, every thing is conducted by Spirits, no less than Digestion or Sleep. [to Note the last words of Jesus, Εδοθη μοι πασα εξουσια εν ουρανω και επι γης]

When this Verse was first dictated to me I consider'd a Monotonous Cadence like that used by Milton & Shakspeare & all writers of English Blank Verse, derived from the modern bondage of Rhyming; to be a necessary and indispensible part of Verse. But I soon found that

in the mouth of a true Orator such monotony was not only awkward, but as much a bondage as rhyme itself. I therefore have produced a variety in every line, both of cadences & number of syllables. Every word and every letter is studied and put into its fit place: the terrific numbers are reserved for the terrific parts—the mild & gentle, for the mild & gentle parts, and the prosaic, for inferior parts: all are necessary to each other. Poetry Fetter'd, Fetters the Human Race! Nations are Destroy'd, or Flourish, in proportion as Their Poetry Painting and Music, are Destroy'd or Flourish! The Primeval State of Man, was Wisdom, Art, and Science.

2. William Blake, *Jerusalem* plate 3 (reproduced from David V. Erdman's typographical edition of *The Complete Poetry and Prose of William Blake*).

Erdman into attempting a translation of the linguistic components of Blake's work only, the lexical and grammatical levels
of its textuality. Erdman's edition understands the importance of the visual component, of course, and many of its textual notes comment on the iconic and visual aspects of
Blake's works. Still, the physique of Blake's work, so crucial
to the original "intentions," has not been translated in the
Erdman edition.

Now many will object that I have chosen a special case,
and that most authors work only with linguistic signifiers.
This is an important point, of course, and I shall try to expand upon it in a moment. Nevertheless, it remains true that
a great many writers, and all poets, appreciate the symbolic
and signifying dimensions of the physical medium through
which (or rather *as* which) the linguistic text is embodied.
The initial example of Arnold testifies to this fact on behalf of
a great many other authors.

I chose Blake as my second example partly to dramatize
the signifying functions which are comprised in the physical
aspects of every book, whether illuminated or not. No one
can read an original Blake text, or a facsimile text, and not be
struck by the following fact: that such work has set in motion
two large signifying codes, the linguistic code (which we tend
to privilege when we study language-based arts like novels
and poetry) and the bibliographical code (which interpreters,
until recently, have largely ignored).

The difference between the "Erdman" Blake and the
"Blake" Blake is fundamentally the difference between the
bibliographical codes which operate in the two works. The
Jerusalem that comes to us in the Blake text (or even in a facsimile of that text) sets up a reading field and a set of interpretive possibilities which are very different from those provided
by Erdman's *Jerusalem*.

But I chose the example of Blake for another and very different reason—not because it so clearly reveals the presence

of bibliographical coding, but because it can so subtly mislead us about the status of those bibliographical codes. To read a Blake text in an original or a facsimile is to be told that "author's intentions" dominate the bibliographical signifiers in the same way that they dominate the linguistic signifiers. And while this is true, to a certain (but very limited) extent, for Blake, it is not true for most authors. Blake is unique in the history of English literature precisely because of his effort to bring every aspect of the signifying process, linguistic as well as bibliographical, under authorial control: in fact, to make the author's intention what many textual critics believe it is and ought to be, the ultimate and sole authority of the entire text.

In the language arts, the author, or authors (if they are multiple), define a text's initial signifiers in the area of linguistics. Other authorities may enter the linguistic text at a later point and introduce important changes—as Erdman, for example, intervened in the descent of Blake's texts. Nonetheless, all such later interventions have to be judged in relation to the initial linguistic determinations. It is this structural situation which justifies the traditional argument in editorial theory that "author's intentions" govern the choice of copy-text.

The weakness of the theory is that it largely ignores the transmissive or communicative aspects of linguistic events. "Copy-text," in modern editorial theory, is always a linguistic text. Traditional textual criticism, with its concentration on the linguistic text, is thus happily married to traditional hermeneutics, which elucidates meaning—which *locates* meaning—entirely in linguistic symbologies.

Bibliographical signifiers, on the other hand, immediately call our attention to other styles and scales of symbolic exchange that every language event involves. Meaning is transmitted through bibliographical as well as linguistic codes. Blake's work forcibly reminds us of this, just as it shows us

Blake's heroic effort to bring the bibliographical signifiers under his complete control. But Blake was not able to do this, as the example of Erdman's text should remind us. Even in his own day, Blake was unable to control every aspect of his work's signifying field. His virtual invisibility in his own period is in no small part the result of his vain quest for total control over the works that bear his name.

As the process of textual transmission expands, whether vertically (i.e., over time), or horizontally (in institutional space), the signifying processes of the work become increasingly collaborative and socialized. Blake's work is an act of resistance to those collaborative inertias as they were undergoing a new expansion at the dawn of the age of mechanical reproduction. Byron's work, on the other hand, has to be understood as in great measure a move to accept and triumph through such collaborative exchanges.

The point is that authors (and authorial intentions) do not govern those textual dimensions of a work which become most clearly present to us in bibliographical forms. Byron wrote *Don Juan*, but from the outset the poem developed along two different signifying lines, and in neither case did Byron's authority or intentions predominate. The two lines are bibliographically defined—on one hand, as the series of authorized printings, which amounted to about two thousand copies at very dear prices; and on the other, the cheap piracies, issued in many tens of thousands at a few shillings. These two sets of texts are very different works, and they meant—and still mean—very different things.

Or consider one of Byron's most famous lyrical poems, the notorious "Fare Thee Well!"[10] While the linguistic text of this work is quite stable, at least three versions of the work were circulated in 1816 when it was written: its first (private) printing, which was authorized; its first publication, completely unauthorized, in a newspaper called *The Champion*; and its first authorized publication late in 1816, in book form, after the work had been through dozens—perhaps scores—of further unauthorized publications, printings, and hand copyings. To this day the work is misunderstood largely because we have lost contact with what is very clearly revealed in those early bibliographical codings: that it is as much a poem of hate and revenge as it is a poem of love and broken-heartedness. The first (private) printing, in fifty copies, was carried out under Byron's instructions as part of his effort to gain power (both psychologically and politically) over his wife during their 1816 marriage separation struggles. The unauthorized newspaper printing by *The Champion*, accompanied by an extensive editorial attack on Byron, used Byron's poem—which was meant for a weapon against his wife—as a weapon against him. The third version, the authorized book publication, was part of Byron's effort to regain some control over the situation. In this he succeeded, to a certain extent, but only at the price of turning his poem over to the reviewers, who were able to comment extensively on Byron's duplicity and the factious situation in general.

The character of the poem's involvements in love and hate shifts with the work's bibliographical changes. Through all those shifts and changes, however, the linguistic text preserves a misleadingly calm appearance.

There are, in other words, several distinct versions of Byron's *Don Juan* and "Fare Thee Well!" but each of these versions has virtually the same linguistic content. This is not at all an unusual turn of events within the textual condition. The questions at issue are how textual criticism shall understand this situation, and how critical editors shall deal with it.

I I

At this point I want to locate these more general issues of textuality in the context of certain specialized disputes about editing and textual theory. This narrower focus is important for two reasons. First, it helps to explain how certain apparently technical problems impinge directly on more general issues of textuality. Second, it sharpens our awareness of just how the textual condition is a scene of contest and interaction, a scene where specific textual decisions are made (or unmade) in a context that involves many people. The actions of these persons, while always collective, are not always consciously or willfully cooperative.

My work has been associated with a so-called social theory of editing. This idea, or this locution, has been understood in a number of ways, not all of them correspondent with what I have stood and argued for. Perhaps these misunderstandings have arisen because of my faulty presentation. Whatever the reason, let me restate here some of my views.

My study of texts—principally but by no means exclusively poems and novels of the past two centuries—has made me aware that literary works are coded bibliographically as well as linguistically. In the case of the bibliographical codes, "author's intentions" rarely control the state or the transmission of the text. In this sense literary texts and their meanings are collaborative events. Some writers enter these collaborations actively and positively—one thinks, for example, of the books of Jack Spicer's poetry, whose physical appearance is so central to their textual meanings. In other cases the collaborations are unsought for, or perhaps even positively resisted. The crossed meanings of "Fare Thee Well!," which Byron did not want spread abroad, are an outstanding example of collaborative textual production. Because editors tend to theorize their texts within "author intentional" models, however, these more complex aspects of textuality are not foregrounded in their work (i.e., in their editions).

If the presence of other textual authorities is apparent in the bibliographical codes, it frequently invades the linguistic codes as well. We observe these kinds of invasions most often, perhaps, when we notice the part which certain readers and editors play in the production of an author's work: when we look, for instance, at Faulkner's printer's copy manuscripts, with their three-way dialogue of textual changes carried on by Faulkner and two of Random House's copy editors. These kinds of collaborative efforts attract our attention because they generally concern the text's linguistic code, which we commonly treat as the work's locus of meaning. In fact, however, the most important "collaboration" process is that which finds ways of marrying a linguistic to a bibliographical text. We confront such marriages most forcefully when we read texts which, while "written by" certain writers, were never "authorized" by them. The production of this kind of text is carried out under the authority, and by the final intentions, of persons other than the writer of the texts. One of the crucial texts of Byron's "Fare Thee Well!" is in fact an unauthorized printing. Its importance, however, does not lie in its linguistic readings, which are virtually identical to its (authorized) copy-text. *The Champion* text is important because of the new set of bibliographical codes (and meanings) which it set in motion.

These nonauthorial interventions are important, theoretically, because they expose the problematic character of the concept of final intentions, which has become so important in twentieth-century editorial theory. The concept represents itself as a determinate as well as a determinable thing, at least theoretically: determinate because it excludes the "nonauthorial," and determinable because a stemma of textual relations can be postulated and constructed.

Authors' relations with their readers and editors, however, are highly interactive. The character of these interactions varies greatly from situation to situation. Because the critical editor's task is to expose and clarify those interactions, theory cannot begin by positing the existence of texts which are purely transmissive mechanisms. Texts are also the locus of complex networks of communicative exchanges, and the first of those exchanges is revealed at the time of a work's initial period of production.

So far as the practice of editing is concerned, this idea of text as a field of communicative exchange does not ask us to discard any of the traditional concepts or tools of editing and textual criticism. It asks us, rather, to reconceive the framework governing the use of those tools and concepts. Thus, although it has been said, not infrequently, that my *Critique of Modern Textual Criticism* discards author's final intentions as a criterion for making decisions about choice of copy-text,[11] the complaint is mistaken. *Critique* explicitly sets forth author's intentions as one of the criteria for making decisions about copy-text. What *Critique* does argue, however—and in this my position departs from what has been the normative one—is that scholars should not use author's intentions as the ultimate and determining criterion for copy-text. Each case has to be judged on its own.[12]

Correlative with this position is the argument that no single editorial procedure—no single "text" of a particular work—can be imagined or hypothesized as the "correct" one, that there are many mansions in the house of editorial choices. The indeterminacy of the textual situation fluctuates in relation to the size and complexity of the surviving body of textual materials: the larger the archive, the greater the room for indeterminacy. And it must be understood that the archive includes not just original manuscripts, proofs, and editions, but all the subsequent textual constitutions which the work undergoes in its historical passages.

Two examples will indicate how and why the concept "author's (final) intentions" cannot be used to determine copy-text. The first is the notorious case of Yeats.[13] Toward the end of his life he was deeply involved, along with his publisher Macmillan, with the project of the so-called De Luxe edition of his complete works. Yeats looked upon this edition as the chance to put the texts of his poems into forms which would represent his "final intentions." In working for such an edition he was doing no more than what many authors have done before and since—one thinks immediately of Swinburne, for example, and James.

For various reasons, however, this project dragged on over many years after its initial conception in 1931. It was not completed at Yeats's death; then, the war intervened and various other complications developed. Richard Finneran's efforts to produce a complete and corrected edition of Yeats's poems raised a storm of scholarly dispute when it finally appeared in 1983. Finneran clearly anticipated some such event, for when he issued his edition he also published an accompanying volume explaining the issues and problems involved in editing Yeats's work.

There is no need to rehearse these matters here. Suffice it to say that no one editing Yeats, given the state of the archive as it is presently known, could use "author's (final) intentions" as the determinative criterion for deciding on copy-text for many, perhaps most, of the poems, and especially the so-called *Last Poems*. Yeats repeatedly worked and reworked the texts of various poems in the 1930s: the scene of writing is one where Yeats (and his editor at Macmillan, Thomas Mark) put many different sets of intentions in motion, and where these intentions often reached no definitive point of resolution.

The situation calls attention to a further problem with the criterion of author's intentions as the guiding rule for deciding on copy-text. I have in mind the problem Hershel Parker likes to raise in his pursuit of what he imagines to be the text that best reveals the author's creativity: that is, do we want first thoughts or last thoughts, first intentions or final intentions? Do we choose, for example, some text associated with the first edition of Swinburne's *Poems and Ballads* (1866), or some text associated with the 1904 collected edition which Swinburne scrupulously worked over?

In such cases we glimpse part of the fundamental ambiguity in the concept of "author's intentions," and hence part of the reason why one might reasonably conclude that the concept cannot be determinative of copy-text in many cases. "Author's intentions," first or final, has to be one among several criteria we use when trying to edit.

But if the concept is indeterminate even within the arena of the author's solitary activities, its indeterminacy multiplies when we remember that authorship is a social and not a solitary act or set of acts. Authorship is a special form of human communicative exchange, and it cannot be carried on without interactions, cooperative and otherwise, with various persons and audiences. In these events editors and publishers function as the means by which a text's interaction with its audience(s) is first objectively hypothesized and tested.

For example, Faulkner's *Absalom, Absalom!* has recently been edited to a text that has used Faulkner's typescript as its copy-text—that is to say, the typescript Faulkner sent to his publisher. The textual result, which calls itself the "corrected text" of the novel, emerged after the customary collations with all the relevant archival material, including the corrected proofs and so forth.[14] The new work is, in fact, a very good textual edition.

Had I been the editor, however, I would probably have used the corrected proofs as my copy-text, and not the typescript; and had the corrected proofs not existed, I should probably have turned to the first edition for my copy-text. I would then have run through the usual collations with the extant archival material, and the result would have been yet another "corrected text" of the novel. It would differ from the "corrected text" that we now have. More significantly, however, because the changes it would have introduced would be different from the changes which were introduced into the other "corrected text," we would be led to realize that what editors call "corrections to a text" denominate a wide range of material. On one end of the scale are plain mistakes—classically, inadvertent typographical or scribal deviations from the exemplar texts. As one moves toward the other end of the scale, however, the category of "corrections" begins to shift into what might be called "informed changes." These "informed changes" are editorial alterations made by the editor, and they can be called "corrections" so long as we understand the term to mean "corrections as they have been imagined and generated through a particular theory of the text."

In the case of *Absalom, Absalom!* the scholarly editor of the "corrected text" has made it his business to override certain earlier editorial interventions—the earlier ones being those that Faulkner and certain of his contemporaries worked cooperatively to produce. One editorial activity thus comes to replace another. In theory this later (scholastic) intervention imagines itself to be a kind of nonactivity functioning only to remove certain earlier interventions in the text. But of course this is a mystification, for the scholar's text radically alters the original textual situation. His intervention into the linguistic text is conscious and acknowledged, and defended as a process of correction rather than of alteration. As we have seen, however, whereas some editorial changes are plainly "corrections," many will be far more problematical and have to be seen for what they are: alterations that aspire to be taken for corrections. Such changes can be no more than scholastic aspirations just because the scholar's text is more removed from the scene of the "author's intentions" than is the first edition, or the printer's copy typescript, or the proofs, and so forth. The scholar's text is a positive construction in its own right, a new stage of collaboration with the (now dead) author and his or her earlier collaborators. Every

65

new edition, including every critical edition, is an act of re-imagining and redefining a text's audience(s) and its ways of interacting with those audience(s).[15]

The point is that author's intentions are always operating along with nonauthorial intentions, that each presupposes the other, and that no text ever came into being, or could come into being, without interactions between the two. The theoretical effort to erase this fundamentally interactive pro-cess—to imagine writing and the production of texts as a soli-tary activity—is not so much mistaken as it is a highly spe-cialized way of imagining the nature of texts. It becomes a mistaken theory only when it represents itself as catholic and comprehensive—when, for example, it imagines "final inten-tions" to be the ultimate and determining criterion of copy-text.

The scholar's edition changes the authoritative work in an-other important respect, however. It produces the work in a bibliographical form that departs more or less drastically from the work as originally produced. The more elaborate and successful the scholarly edition—for instance, Erdman's edition of Blake, Jared Curtis's edition of Wordworth's 1807 *Poems*, or several of the so-called Norton critical editions (like the edition of *Bleak House*)—the more sharply it is likely to depart from the original authoritative texts; and the departure will be drastic no matter which of the originary texts one chooses to take as "copy-text."

Where, then, does this discussion of the problems of edi-torial theory leave us? Three important conclusions have emerged.

First, a careful distinction must be drawn between the lin-guistic and the bibliographical features of text. The distinc-tion is important because it highlights the interactive nature of textuality as such. So far as editors are concerned, the chief (but not sole) authority over the linguistic text is the author, whereas the chief (but not sole) authority over the bibliographical text normally falls to the publishing institution within which an author is working.

Second, both linguistic and bibliographical texts are symbolic and signifying mechanisms. Each generates meaning, and while the bibliographical text commonly functions in a subordinate relation to the linguistic text, "meaning" in literary works results from the exchanges these two great semiotic mechanisms work with each other. (On this point I shall have much more to say in the next chapter.)

Third, if one focusses on the narrower issue of the linguistic text alone, one arrives at certain conclusions with respect to the editorial problem of copy-text and authorial intentions. Today the normative theory is that copy-text should be determined by the criterion of author's intentions. However, that theory is based upon a concept—"author's intentions"—which is itself ambiguous and unstable. Furthermore, the concept as it has evolved in editorial theory misrepresents the interactive procedures by which texts are constituted, including the critical texts generated out of the editorial theory of author's intentions.

Let me close by returning to the question posed at the outset, "What is critical editing?" To respond to that question I have been drawing examples from the modern periods; but, if the "eclectic" theory of critical editing were applied to the investigation of a great many earlier texts, its inadequacy would be quickly exposed. Medieval scholars are especially aware of its deficiencies; but if we imagine trying to edit Donne, or Raleigh, or Rochester according to an eclectic theory of critical editing, we quickly find ourselves in the position which the eclectic tradition left the editing of Shakespeare.[16]

Shakespeare's texts are now undergoing a massive critical reexamination and the process has come to involve the critical reimagination of critical editing itself. We confront a scene where multiple texts are common, and where categories like "good" and "bad" quartos are dissolving. In the event, eclectic editing has been revealed as no more than one possible form of critical editing, and a form which is subject to serious limitations, including that ultimate limitation: the knowledge that in many cases its employment would mean the very opposite of "critical."

3

The Socialization of Texts

ELEVEN YEARS ago G. Thomas Tanselle published an influential essay for scholars, "The Editing of Historical Documents." This paper was written as a strong, if also a friendly, critique of postwar work in historical editing. Tanselle argued that historical editing had, in general, been based upon an inadequate understanding of the nature of text. In this regard, according to Tanselle, many distinguished historical editing projects lagged far behind analogous projects undertaken by literary scholars. The problem was that historical editors, in contrast to their literary counterparts, had been too "apt to neglect the physical form in which the evidence on which they subsist has been preserved."[1]

This judgment must have come as a surprise to most historical editors, since the nature of their principal material—its documentary character—forces them to encounter the physique of their texts in ways that many literary editors do not experience. But Tanselle showed that historical editors were making excessive interventions into the documents being edited, changing text in misguided and often contradictory efforts to deliver the material in more efficient or accessible ways.

Today few people—certainly not I—would disagree with Tanselle's plea that editors should give the greatest respect to the physical integrity of the documents. Most of what I wish to argue here will involve an extrapolation of Tanselle's plea.

But to the extent that Tanselle's essay focussed on the editing of manuscript-based materials, his representation of the problems confronting literary editors can be misleading.

The heart of his theoretical argument rests in his insistence that no sharp distinction should be made in the editorial policy applied to historical and to literary texts: "No clear line can be drawn between writing which is 'literature' and writing which is not" (495), Tanselle says, and he adduces various examples, all very much—so far as they go—to the point. He then adds, however, that "a distinction does need to be made, not between literary and historical materials [but between] works intended for publication and private papers" (496). Tanselle gives about one-third of a single page to a discussion of this important matter—his essay is fifty-six pages long—and then proceeds to say that "this is not the place to explore" the distinction he has drawn. "The point here," he remarks, "is to contrast that situation [i.e., text involved in a publishing venue] with the very different one which exists for private documents" (497).

When Tanselle rejects the distinction between a historical and a literary document—between informational and aesthetic works—he sets a gulf between himself and a textual theorist like Hershel Parker. Parker is aware, I am sure, that a historical work can be pursued or considered within an aesthetic horizon. Gibbon's *Decline and Fall* is probably as much a work of art as it is a work of history. He must be equally aware that literary works always disseminate historical information. Nonetheless, Parker, like Aristotle, would not want to collapse the distinction between these two kinds of work because they epitomize the difference between a form of writing that is committed to facticity and information, and a form that is, by contrast, devoted to creation.

History and literature differ, that is to say, along the line of their intentionalities. This being the case, we find in Parker's work a passionate engagement with the issue of literary intention. Parker's insistence that editors of literary works should return to authorial manuscripts wherever possible represents his desire to position the text in as close a relation to its authoritative source as possible. For literary work, in this view, is the creative expression of an individual's quest for meaning and order. The scholarly editor's task is to clarify as much as one can the artistic process of creative activity, for it is that process which *is* the literary work, whether we look at the work as a carrier of meaning (informational) or as a creative event (aesthetic).

Furthermore, if Parker, in contrast to Tanselle, maintains a clear distinction between historical and literary work, he reverses Tanselle's text-theoretical distinction between private papers and public (normally, for our period, printed) texts. Tanselle takes the distinction as a sign that some texts (typically, "creative works") seek wide dissemination and a kind of iconic perfection, whereas others (typically, private documents) do not. But for Parker, the question of dissemination through printing is secondary, if not irrelevant, to the primary issue of artistic creativity.

For this reason Parker argues that Bowers and Tanselle are confused on the issue of intentionality. Their confusion is most apparent in the value they set upon so-called eclectic editing. To proceed with an editorial process along those lines is, for Parker, at best to court and at worst to ensure an unhappy result. The eclectic edition is by definition *not* a single authorial construct but a polyglot formation imagined by the editor. Furthermore, if the eclectic edition is based on a printed version of the work rather than an authorial manuscript version, the result will be to move even further from that moment "when the artist was most in control" of his own work.[2]

I detail these matters here in order to position my argument with respect to this seminal debate. In what follows, therefore, I shall be trying to explain why I stand with Parker

(and against Tanselle) in maintaining the distinction between historical and literary work, and why I support Tanselle (as against Parker) in Tanselle's view of the distinction
between private and public documents. My own view of literary work, and hence of how to go about editing it, rests on
this pair of distinctions. Furthermore, the distinctions highlight the centrality of literary texts for understanding the textual condition.

II

I have no disagreement with Parker, or Bowers, or Tanselle
on a great many issues of editorial procedure. I take it we all
agree that no scholarly editing can take place which does not
enumerate all the relevant texts and establish their genetic or
collateral relations. We also agree that all such information
should be made available to readers who wish to judge both
the nature and the executive adequacy of the edition. On
other technical matters we differ. We do not agree, for instance, on the criteria for establishing copy-text; we also differ, in various ways, on the appropriateness of copy-text editing (which is to say, "eclectic" editing) for different kinds of
text.

But these are not the subjects I mean to discuss here.
Rather, I want to explore a pair of topics that expose the kind
of approach I take toward editing literary works. The first
deals with the question of multiple artistic intentionalities.
The second concerns the aesthetic dimension of documentary
materials.

Contemporary text theory, in the arena of literary scholarship, founded itself (as we saw in the last chapter) on the idea
of authorial intentions. No one, of course, repudiates either
the reality or the importance of authorial intentionality for
the problem of text theory or editorial method. What is at
issue is how absolutely the concept of authorial intention is
to be understood *so far as the editing of literary works is*

concerned. For Parker, the sole criterion on which a literary-editorial project ought to be based is the criterion of authorial intention. Furthermore, Parker postulates for every literary work an ideal process of creation. This process may become diverted or corrupted in many ways, by the author or by any number of other agents. The editor's task is to cut through those diversions and corruptions in order to reveal, as purely as possible, the original artist's creative intention.

Bowers and Tanselle also base their editorial theories on the concept of authorial intention. But because they discern in the production of literary works the presence of multiple authorial intentions, they seek to make compromises between the options offered by the diversity of textual witnesses. These compromises appear as the eclectic edition, which is an editorial construction built up from a copy-text. That copy-text becomes "eclectic" when the editor, after examining the relevant documents, introduces readings from other textual witnesses which are judged to exhibit greater authority than the authority of the copy-text.

Parker criticizes the eclectic approach because it violates his notion of artistic integrity. The creative process for him is the artist's rage for order, which cannot be well approximated when an editor seeks for rationally derived compromises. It succeeds least of all if an editor grants equal authority to printed as to manuscript materials. In this situation, Parker devalues printed texts because they cannot embody the integrity of the artist's vision—too many other agents are involved in the production of such work. The job of the editor is to rescue the work from the chaos of conflicting and secondary authorities and agents—including the author's own secondary thoughts.

Eclectic editors, for their part, observe the scene somewhat differently. Where Parker sees randomness obscuring a hidden wholeness, the eclectic editor observes a kind of textual solar system, with the famous "copy-text" standing as the center of gravity around which many textual planets move and have their being. "Copy-text" is the still point in the turning world of a diversity of secondary or dependent texts.

But suppose the textual condition does not correspond to either of these imaginings. Suppose, for example, that the textual condition were to appear in the likeness of D. G. Rossetti's poetic sequence *The House of Life*. This work, as we have seen, was produced in multiple versions. Some of these versions stand in a genetic line of relation with each other, and hence could be taken for the dependencies of a primary authority. But one of the versions does not stand in such a relation, and the work breaks up into other kinds of independent units within each of the larger versions. Besides, the standard version of this work is a posthumous editorial construction made up from a decision about how to treat the heterodox amalgam of textual deposits.

Multiple versions of many Shakespeare works also come down to us—most notoriously, *King Lear*—and this situation is not merely common in the case of theatrical work, it is the rule. Today, the very concept of the famous "bad quartos," once firmly established in editorial treatment of Shakespeare, has been undermined. Furthermore, it is equally typical that alterations in the texts of plays are the consequence of the collective efforts of the theatrical company. Texts change under the pressure of immediate events.

Charles Lamb's highly artistic essays—they are really types of prose poem—appear as one thing when they are first published in *The London Magazine*, and as quite other things when he moves to have them produced in book form. The Cuala Press editions of Yeats's poems differ sharply from the texts brought out (almost at the same time) under the Macmillan imprint.

But there is no call to multiply examples. The problem is well known. Let me just conclude with the startling case of Ezra Pound's last published installment of his *Cantos* project, the section known as *Drafts and Fragments*. Here it is not merely that an extreme indeterminacy governs the state of the texts. More difficult is the fact, now well documented, that various agents besides Pound were involved in the production of this work.[3] I should also make it clear that this case is just an extreme instance of something one discovers repeatedly in literary studies. Traditional ballads and songs typically descend to us through wildly heterodox lines of textual transmission. In such cases, trying to edit on the basis of any concept of "authorial intention" or "authorial control" is simply impossible.

Of course, each of these versions may be usefully studied as a singular example of a creative process, as may the two texts of *King Lear*, or the multiple versions of Stoppard's plays. Literary editing should encourage that kind of study. Nevertheless, literary work by its very nature sets in motion many kinds of creative intentionalities. These orbit in the universe of the creative work—but not around some imaginary and absolute center. Rather, they turn through many different kinds of motion, at many structural scales, and in various formal relationships. The universe of poiesis no more has an absolute center than does the stellar universe we have revealed through our astronomy. What it has are many relative centers which are brought to our attention by our own acts of observation. The universe of literature is socially generated and does not exist in a steady state. Authors themselves do not have, *as authors*, singular identities; an author is a plural identity and more resembles what William James liked to call the human world at large, a multiverse.

Literary texts differ from informational texts by being polyvocal. Whereas "noise" is always a form of corruption for a channel of information, it can be exploited in literary texts for positive results. The thicker the description, so far as an artist is concerned, the better. (Minimalist styles of art thicken their media by processes of subtraction and absence.)

A thickened text is a scene where metaphor and metonymy thrive (Coleridge's "opposite or discordant qualities," his "sameness with difference"). For Parker, the thickness comes from the artists' imaginative resources, who can be counted on to put into their texts far more than even they are aware of. Parker's "intention" includes, crucially, the vast resources of the unconscious and preconscious.

But thickness is also built through the textual presence and activities of many nonauthorial agents. These agencies may be the artist's contemporaries—these are the examples most often adduced—or they may not; furthermore, the agencies may hardly be imagined as "individuals" at all. The texts of Sappho, for example, gain much of their peculiar power from their fragmented condition, and the same is true for various ballads and songs, which exploit their textual fractures and absences for poetic results.

Most important of all, however, so far as the *aesthesis* of texts is concerned, are the scholars and institutions of transmission who hand our cultural deposits down to us. Texts emerge from these workshops in ever more rich and strange forms. Indeed, readers sometimes complain that cultural transmitters interfere with the original texts too much, that they make them appear too difficult, too alien—too thick and encumbered. And no doubt there are many helpless and hopeless interventions. But who is to say for certain which they are? Besides, "literary" work, in its textual condition, is not meant for transparency, is not designed to carry messages. Messages may be taken from such work, but always and only by acts of simplification and diminishment. So readers, in those ghostly shapes we call critics and scholars, hear many voices in the texts they study. Like Tennyson's sea, what is literary "moans round" with many such voices. In doing and being so, texts put the features of textuality on fullest display.

76

I I I

To this point I have been taking the word "text" to signify the linguistic text, the verbal outcome at every level (from the most elementary forms of single letters and punctuation marks up to the most complex rhetorical structures that comprise the particular linguistic event). And even if we agree, for practical purposes, to restrict the term "text" to this linguistic signification, we cannot fail to see that literary works typically secure their effects by other than purely linguistic means. Every literary work that descends to us operates through the deployment of a double helix of perceptual codes: the linguistic codes, on one hand, and the bibliographical codes on the other.

We recognize the latter simply by *looking* at a medieval literary manuscript—or at any of William Blake's equivalent illuminated texts produced in (the teeth of) the age of mechanical reproduction. Or at Emily Dickinson's manuscript books of poetry, or her letters. In each of these cases the physique of the "document" has been forced to play an aesthetic function, has been made part of the "literary work." That is to say, in these kinds of literary works the distinction between physical medium and conceptual message breaks down completely.

I could adduce scores of similar examples of works generated out of the production mechanisms developed by printing institutions. The most obvious are the ornamental texts produced, for example, by writers like William Morris, but the books published by Whitman, Yeats, W. C. Williams, and Pound—to name only the most obvious examples—make the same point. Less apparent, but no less significant, are the novels of Dickens and Thackeray, or the serial fictions produced throughout the nineteenth century—topics I shall elaborate upon in a moment. If Tanselle cannot easily draw a distinction between a historical and a literary work, it is just as difficult to distinguish, in all these cases, between that which is documentary and that which is literary. The physical presentation of these printed texts has been made to serve aesthetic ends.

Textual and editorial theory has heretofore concerned itself almost exclusively with the linguistic codes. The time has come, however, when we have to take greater theoretical account of the other coding network which operates at the documentary and bibliographical level of literary works.

Not that scholars have been unaware of the existence of these bibliographical codes. We have simply neglected to incorporate our knowledge into our theories of text. Surely no editor of Coleridge's "The Rime of the Ancient Mariner"—if the editor chose to print the 1816 rather than the 1798 text— would consider placing the famous set of glosses anywhere except in the margin of the work. The glosses have to be *there*, and not set as either footnotes or endnotes, because their bibliographical position is in itself highly meaningful. Placed as they are, the glosses make an important historical allusion that affects the work in the most profound way. A similar kind of historical allusion operates in the ink, typeface, and paper used by William Morris in the first edition of his *The Story of the Glittering Plain* (1891). Both involve literary allusions: the one to medieval conventions of textual glossing, the other to fifteenth-century styles of typography and book production.

As Tanselle has argued, every documentary or bibliographical aspect of a literary work is meaningful, and potentially significant. But Tanselle's clear, practical sense of this matter has not led him to imagine how such materials are to be incorporated into a theory of texts and editing. On the contrary, in fact. He has neglected doing so, I believe, not because of his adherence to an eclectic model of editing, but because of his unnecessarily restricted view of the processes of literary signification.

A few more examples will clarify what I have in mind. In the current controversy over the edition of *Ulysses*, attention has been focussed on a number of specialized, and largely executive, issues (for example, the *Ulysses'* editors failure to work directly from original documents rather than from photocopies).[4] The overriding editorial question, however, has always been this: Should Gabler have chosen the 1922 *Ulysses* as copy-text instead of trying to construct as his copy-text (if that is the right term in this peculiar case) the theoretical entity he called in his edition "the continuous manuscript text?" Without going into the technical issues involved, let me simply observe that John Kidd—Gabler's chief critic—originally took his own preference for the 1922 edition because he detected in that book an elaborate symbolism keyed to the sequence of page numbers. If Joyce's page numbering has been symbolically deployed, that fact has to be registered in the editorial reconstruction. Specifically, the 1922 pagination of *Ulysses* would have to be editorially preserved.

The example of *Ulysses* ought to remind us that many of the key works of the modernist movement in literature, especially the work produced before 1930, heavily exploit the signifying power of documentary and bibliographical materials. The first thirty of Pound's *Cantos*, published in three book installments between 1925 and 1930, are only the most outstanding examples of this fact about modernist texts. A great many similar examples could be cited from modernist writers working all across the Euro-American literary scene.

Nor does the situation change if we move back in time. The case of Thackeray is well known and typical, and the particular example of *Vanity Fair* eloquent. In the first 1848 edition Thackeray himself designed the sixty-six decorated

79

initials and eighty-three vignettes—as well, of course, as the thirty-eight principal illustrations. His surviving manuscript of the novel with his markups shows where he wanted various cuts to appear. Yet most editions of *Vanity Fair* omit these materials altogether, even though they are clearly involved in the structure of the book's meaning. Gordon Ray has pointed out, for example, that while the verbal text "leaves unanswered the question of whether or not Becky Sharp brought about the death of Jos Sedley[,] his etching of Becky's second appearance in the character of Clytemnestra more than hints that she did."[5] Thackeray's decorated cover for the nineteen separate parts of the serially published text (1847–48) is an equally unmistakable case of the book's graphic materials being coded for significance. Indeed, in chapter 8 of the novel the narrator refers to that symbolic design and explicates its meaning.[6]

From a scholarly point of view, it would be difficult to justify an edition of Thackeray that omits the illustrative matter handled at the documentary level of the work. For the novel is not merely "one of the best illustrated books in the world," it is also an important "experiment in composite form as much as Edward Lear's *Book of Nonsense*" (1846)[7]—as much, indeed, as the more famous "composite art" of William Blake. Indeed, Thackeray explicitly calls attention to his own composite art in the subtitle of his novel: "Pen (i.e., linguistic) and Pencil (i.e., graphic) Sketches of English Society."

Yet the same must be said in the case of Dickens, even though Dickens did not, like Blake, Thackeray, and Lear, design his own illustrations. For the texts of Dickens's novels were equally produced as works of composite art, though in this case Dickens supplied only the pen, while others worked with the pencil. The relevance of the illustrative material has been acknowledged throughout the editorial history of Dickens's works, both their scholarly and their commercial history.

Or what would one say of a critical edition of the Alice books that omitted the designs of Sir John Tenniel? So important was Tenniel's work for the first of the Alice books (*Alice's Adventures in Wonderland*, 1865) that his protest at the poor printing of the first edition caused the book to be cancelled altogether.

In fact, we have two distinct versions of this famous book: the version on which Carroll and Tenniel collaborated, published in 1865, and the fair manuscript copy with Carroll's own illustrations made as a Christmas gift for Anne Liddell, and eventually published in 1886. In both cases the verbal text and the documentary materials operate together to a single literary result.

Nor do I mean to isolate for importance, in the case of this work, only the marriage of illustration and text. As Tenniel's protest over the poor printing of the first edition indicates, the entire documentary level of the work must be understood as carrying significance. The fact that one version was conceived as a publishing event, and the other as a manuscript gift book, sets the bibliographical coding for each version on an entirely different footing.

The two versions of *Alice's Adventures in Wonderland* may well remind us of the variant versions of so many nineteenth-century books, especially the novels. Serial publication of one kind or another was the rule, as were the related publication mechanisms we associate with institutions like the circulating library. Writers worked within those particular sets of circulatory conventions (though they vary with place and time, such conventions always exist) and the literary results— the books issued—are coded for meaning accordingly.

Furthermore, different types of serialization were available. A novel written for weekly serial publication, like Dickens's *Hard Times* (1854),[8] is not merely *written* differently from one that is written for monthly circulation (or for no serial publication at all); it is *produced* differently and comes into the reader's view via differently defined bibliographical structures of meaning. Or consider the exemplary case of *Oliver Twist*. First issued in serial parts in the monthly magazine *Bentley's Miscellany* (1837–39), it was printed again in three volumes (1838) even before the serial run had been concluded. Then in 1846 it was published again, this time in ten serial installments (the run in *Bentley's Miscellany* had been twenty-four installments). In each of these cases the text is organized very differently. The *Bentley's* and the three volume publications comprise fifty-one chapters, whereas the 1846 serial publication has fifty-three. *Bentley's* is divided into three "Books," but these do not correspond exactly to the three "volumes" of 1838. The *Bentley's* serial typically prints two, sometimes three chapters per unit, whereas the monthly numbered parts of 1846 typically contain six, sometimes five (and in one case, four) chapters.[9]

These kinds of production structures can be exploited for aesthetic effects in particular and always highly individuated ways. *Pickwick Papers* first appeared in serial parts (1836–37), as did *Little Dorrit* (1855–57), but in each case the bibliographical codes are manipulated to unique effect. The latter is one of the late novels, produced twenty years after the groundbreaking effort of *Pickwick Papers*. The early work is far more episodic than the later, so much so that many would be reluctant to call *Pickwick Papers* a novel at all. Whatever it is, the work emerged through the mutual efforts of Dickens, two illustrators (Robert Seymour and Hablot Knight Browne ["Phiz"]), and the production mechanisms set in motion by the publishers Chapman and Hall, all working together in cooperative consultation.[10]

Literary works are distinct from other linguistic forms in their pursuit of extreme concrete particularity. That special feature of "literature" has two consequences we all recognize. First, literary works tend toward textual and bibliographical dispersion (signalled at the earliest phases of the work by authorial changes of direction and revision, which may continue for protracted periods). Second, they are committed to work via the dimension of *aesthesis* (i.e., via the materiality of experience that Blake called "the doors of perception" and that Morris named "resistance"). In each case, literary works tend to multiply themselves through their means and modes of production. These processes of generation are executed in the most concrete and particular ways. *Oliver Twist* is produced during Dickens's lifetime in several important creative forms. But then there are equally important versions of that work—equally significant from an aesthetic point of view—that are produced later. Kathleen Tillotson's is a splendid edition of a great literary work, but perhaps we should want to argue that her edition is not the work of Charles Dickens. And perhaps we should be right in doing so.

Tillotson's edition stands in relation to Dickens's novel in the same kind of relation that (say) the Tate Gallery stands to the paintings of Turner. Both gallery and edition force us to engage with artistic work under a special kind of horizon. It is far from the horizon under which Dickens and Turner originally worked. It is nonetheless, still, an aesthetic and literary horizon, and that fact cannot be forgotten. Of course we cannot recover the earlier frame of reference; all we can do is make imaginative attempts at reconstituting or approximating it for later persons living under other skies. The vaunted immortality sought after by the poetic impulse will be achieved, if it is achieved at all, in the continuous socialization of the texts.

IV

We cannot leave this subject without making one last critical turn upon the idea of textual socialization. I have in mind a subject implicitly raised by my examples of the museum and the scholarly edition. The problem appears if we simply give this pair of cultural formats their more demonic names: the white cube, and the tome.[11] Brian O'Doherty meticulously detailed how "Context [i]s Content" in the museum, the gallery, and the exhibition.[12] The same is true of any critical edition—indeed, and as I have already tried to show, of any book or printed form whatever.

O'Doherty's is, however, a worried and deconstructive study of "Context as Content." In this respect it resembles some recent ethnographic works—for example, James Clifford's *The Predicament of Culture: Twentieth-Century Literature, Ethnography, and Art*.[13] This entire tradition of critical reflection—to which I myself have contributed, in the domain of literature, with *The Romantic Ideology*[14]—seeks to expose the concealed, and often nonconscious, ideological purposes and assumptions of certain institutional and systematic forms.

Ideology-critique is not, however, the only object of this kind of analysis. We see this alternative impulse in the following passage from Clifford, for example:

> While the object systems of art and anthropology are institutionalized and powerful, they are not immutable. The categories of the beautiful, the cultural, and the authentic have changed and are changing. Thus it is important to resist the tendency of collections to be self-sufficient, to suppress their own historical, economic, and political processes of production. . . . Ideally the history of its own collection and display should be a visible aspect of any exhibition. (229)

I shall have more to say about this call to resistance in a moment. For now, however, I want to point out how the editors of critical editions might argue that their work meets Clifford's demands.

The critical edition is obliged, by its most ancient rules, to place "the history of its own" texts on full display. That is to say, as I pointed out in the previous chapter, a complete apparatus criticus for the text is a sine qua non of the critical edition. However, precisely because the bibliographical codes of books have not been customarily imagined as part of the critical editor's project, scholarly editions have rarely exposed the hidden ideological histories which are imbedded in the documentary forms of transmitted texts, including the documentary form (that squashed paper cube) called the critical edition. If Clifford's revisionist program were to be followed by literary scholars, the bibliographical codes of the texts would have to be made a major object of historical analysis—as important for the critical edition as the apparatus criticus is for its linguistic codes. This would be a major new undertaking for textual scholars. Indeed, it would involve, I believe, a project of greater critical significance for textual scholarship than anything we have seen since the even more epochal breakthroughs of the late eighteenth century.

But there is a sense in which any device that calls the reader's attention to the constructed nature of texts contains an implicit or possible "mode of resistance to the literary work of art." When William Morris began his aggressive assault on the drab transparency of nineteenth-century books, his project was not simply an attempt to retreat from "six counties overhung with smoke." It was also an effort to call attention to what those counties were doing to the art and society of imperial England. The work turned out of the Kelmscott Press, like Blake's illuminated texts of one hundred years before, were meant to produce what Brecht would later call an "alienation effect." The artisanal features of Morris's books declared themselves as made things. Suddenly letters and words were not simply counters to be manipulated for the presentation of those more important things, ideas. The letters and words were dragged back to a new presence, as if incised on the page in an apocalypse of their materiality.

In Morris's great project, language itself began to return to its senses. As a consequence, certain other, larger issues—

social and political issues—were brought to the foreground of the reader's attention. Morris's bibliographical codes did not merely put a frame around his poetical texts, calling attention to their imaginative constructedness. Nor was it simply that the artistic life of Morris's world could be put to shame by a set of brilliant strategic allusions to the bookish arts of the Middle Ages and the early Renaissance. Much more was displayed through the simple but eloquent apparitions of those carefully printed books. The bibliographical self-consciousness of his works exposed the enormous historical deficit which yawned within the apparent wealth of late nineteenth-century English imperial resources.

The example of Morris—Blake or Dickinson would have served as well—exposes a further range of possibilities for the socialized text. When the documentary features of writing are "labelled" (as Brecht might say) in literary works, a "context" for the text's linguistic system (its erstwhile "content") is symbolically invoked. The documentary features may identify that context more or less fully, more or less clearly. It is unmistakable in Morris, whose socialism—in all its dramatic and even shocking contradictions—is written across the pages of the books he published from 1889 onwards (not all of them Kelmscott Press books, not all of them his own).

In Blake and Dickinson—as the reception history of the one, and the textual history of the other, shows—the documents are more elusive and secretive. Both have had to be slowly and meticulously decoded. We know a good deal now about Blake's socialized texts, after more than one hundred years of detailed and continuous investigation. Dickinson's texts, however, despite her enormous popularity as a poet, have yet to be even minimally socialized. The fine editions of Johnson and Franklin lifted Dickinson out of her initial bibliographical gentilities, but so much more needs to be done.[15] A clear ideological reading and critique of the history of her printed texts is essential, but it has not been undertaken. In the end, the full significance of Dickinson's writing will begin to appear when we explicate in detail the importance of the different papers she used, her famous "fascicles," her scripts and their conventions of punctuation and page layout. Many of these fundamental matters remain largely mysterious to this day. Because she is, along with Whitman, one of the two foundational poets of North America, this obscurity at the very heart of her work reflects a grave cultural ignorance—an ignorance all the more dismal for having gone so unnoticed for so long.[16]

4

The Textual Condition

TODAY is Monday, April 1—April Fools' Day. In less than three weeks I shall leave here (Pasadena, California) for Charlottesville, Virginia to attend a conference on textual studies; then I will leave Charlottesville for New York City where I am obliged to address the Society for Textual Scholarship (STS) conference with (perhaps) the remarks you are hearing now, today.

Of course "today" is Saturday, April 27. I write this last statement knowing it to be incorrect—today is *in fact* April Fools' Day—but in the hope that it will one day be true. This hope consoles me, though it carries as well an awful consequence. It is a hope which, if fulfilled, will render incorrect the first sentences I was just writing. Today is not April 1, and I am not in Pasadena. I am not going to Charlottesville; I have already been there.

I am an April fool; I am clearly confused. But it is not my fault, because I have been asked to do an impossible thing: to comment summarily on all the work done at the STS conference. This task is impossible—I have realized this today, April Fools' Day—partly because the variety of work done for the conference is too great. But that is not the most important reason. More important is that here and now (wherever and whenever—April 1, April 27, or any other time) I have only certain uncertain versions of all the relevant texts. I am textually indeterminate, a sort of undocumented alien. This last reason—my current (anytime) state of textual indeterminacy—is interesting because it exemplifies the scholastic version of what ordinary mortals have called "the human condition." I am currently in—deeply in—the textual condition. And I am in it whether I am writing on April 1 or speaking on April 27. Indeed, the textual condition is positively defined by some specific type of indeterminacy analogous to the one I experience at this (whichever) moment.

This is your condition as well since it is the condition of everyone who has to deal in any way with texts—listening to remarks like these, editing books, writing commentaries. But on April 1 I am made acutely conscious of the textual condition because it has assumed a highly specific form. This form is at once circumstantial and teleological. On April 1 it occurs to me that mine is an exemplary case.

Let me review the situation, summarize it, in anticipation of the summary I will give later, on April 27—the summary I am giving now.

Today is April 1 and I have the following documents:

1. The program of the conference in which thirty-eight papers are set down as scheduled for delivery at the STS conference.

2. Eight papers in versions which represent themselves as complete in some sense. In addition, there are three other documents which *may* represent complete papers, though they could also be summaries or narrativized abstracts.

3. Seven abstracts of papers. In addition, I have a document which is called an "abstract" by the author but which is so long and elaborate that it appears to be a finished piece of work in some sense. And another document is ambiguous: it may be an abstract; it may be a complete paper.

4. Four documents which are difficult to categorize. They are neither complete papers nor abstracts, but they indicate—each in a different way—the nature of the material which the authors propose (I shall not say "intend") to take up in their STS presentations.

In my documents on this April Fools' Day, then, I have

twenty-four items which unequivocally represent some authorized stage of development for the thirty-eight STS conference papers: assuming that there will be thirty-eight papers, as is indicated in my other important document, the program. I also have two documents which may or may not represent some authorized version of STS conference papers.

I am charged to say something sensible about the work of this conference taken as a whole. Because the conference director, Don Reiman, is a knowledgeable person, he sent me the documents (all but two of them) which I have already noted. (So much for the matter of provenance.) He sent them because he knew—if I were to be able to say something sensible—I would have to be able to think over the work of the conference, to reflect upon it.

At least I think that this is what I am charged to do. And this is also what I think the existence of these documents means. I may be wrong, however, since the documentation on these questions is somewhat vague and uncertain.

Between now, April 1, and now, April 27, I will produce my remarks on the 1985 STS conference. And I will begin with the materials I have just described.

Well, it is now April 2 and I am no longer an April fool. The foregoing I wrote yesterday, and I propose to carry on from there. Eventually—you may be sure—I will finish this project and you will have the complete text: or at least the orally transmitted version of the complete text. Let us say, *a* complete text, though not necessarily the one I "intended."

This morning, April 2, the body of my documentation remains the same. But this afternoon, April 2, matters are very different. I have received a packet of materials from Indiana relating to the conference in Charlottesville. In this packet are two disturbing documents:

1. A German text of one of the seven abstracts noted in the previous documentation (the abstract is in English). Or at least this German text *appears* to be what the abstract de-

scribes. The author of this document is to give a paper at the conference in Charlottesville. The title of the Charlottesville paper is unknown to me, whereas I have a title for the STS paper. They may or may not be the same.

2. An English text of a paper that carries a different title from the one announced in the STS program, but that may well be the same paper. It is by another author who will appear on the programs of both the Charlottesville and the STS conferences. I do not know the title of his Charlottesville paper. The two texts may or may not be the same. I have only this one document.

These two documents have altered my circumstances considerably, as I now find that I must do some research in another archive altogether: my files on the Charlottesville conference, where I have certain letters and related documents that may throw some light on the contents of these two new texts and their relation to the STS papers. My search reveals one text, of minimal (apparent) significance: a schematic outline of the Charlottesville conference participants along with some notes indicating what some of them may or will speak about. I find that the second of these new papers is not referred to at all by any of these Charlottesville documents. But the paper in German is given a tentative title, in English. The latter does not correspond to either of the titles I already possess.

On this day, April 2, I know more, but I am also more uncertain. But I am still a very happy person. My documentation has grown, including the structure of that documentation. I have had time to think more about the issues, and to think in new ways, from new perspectives. And most of all I am actually producing my text. I have written more than four pages. How splendid.

It is now April 3 and I sit down at my word processor and invoke the text I have been working on for two days for the STS conference. I call up the file and begin reading. I do not like everything I have produced. I start to revise, things disappear forever from the screen and my eyes. I will eventually forget them. You will never know them. If I didn't note their existence here you would never have known of them at all.

Another day passes and I don't know how to go on. I reread the documents I have and for two days I think about them. April 7 arrives; I am back at the word processor. I know what I want to say and I work furiously all morning. I finish my paper for STS. I am happy. I hit the function keys that will save my work.

PANIC AND FEAR. The machine delivers its most dreadful message: BDOS ERROR. I freeze. I have not saved the morning's work (I was inspired; I could not pause to interrupt the flow of the thoughts). I cannot save the file, I cannot exit the file, I can do nothing but strike the RETURN key ineffectually.

It is clear. I am about to lose the morning's work. The first completed text of my paper for the STS conference is lost forever. I will eventually run the corrupted file through my recovery programs and get back, in return for my trouble, fragmented bits of those once beautiful sentences and paragraphs. I wish my machine were alive. I would like to kill it.

April 9 comes and I feel less lost than my lost, inspired prose. I will rewrite the conclusion, and I begin again. This is what I am writing:

> April 7 arrives, I am back at the word processor. I know what I want to say and I work furiously all morning. I finish my paper for STS. I am happy. I hit the function keys that will save my work.
>
> PANIC AND FEAR. The machine delivers its most dreadful message: BDOS ERROR.

Is this what I intended to write? Or perhaps what I *was intending* to write? How strange. I wonder, now, if someone told me that they could reproduce my lost lovely prose, would I want it back? Yes, of course. What scholar would not? But then, would I want it for the conclusion of this text? I don't know. What would I do, in that case, with my *new* conclusion—the one I never intended to write, but did? My mind drifts happily in thoughts of variant readings and parallel texts.

Two more days and we come to the moral of this story. I feel that I am ready to produce a definitive text, to make a definitive statement. It is April 9 and I want to say:

ALL TEXTS ARE PRODUCED OVER TIME AND UNDER VARYING CIRCUMSTANCES.

And I want to say:

ALL TEXTS ARE SOCIALLY AND HISTORICALLY RELATIVE, INCLUDING ALL META-TEXTS SUCH AS SCHOLARLY COMMENTARIES AND EDITIONS.

And I also want to say:

THESE TWO STATEMENTS REFLECT MY UNDER-STANDING AND EXPERIENCE OF TEXTS PRODUCED FOR THE STS CONFERENCE, 1985.

Finally, I shall say this:

IF TEXTS ARE TO BE PRODUCED CRITICALLY, WHETHER THROUGH WRITER, READER, OR EDITOR (ALONG WITH THEIR SURROGATES), THE TEXTS MUST EMPHASIZE THEIR RELATIONS, AND THEIR RELATIVITIES.

Today is April 17. I remain happy with my definitive statements; I no longer wish to revise what I have already produced of this text—except in a few local areas where I make minor alterations and small, rhetorical flourishes. Accidentals, let us say. (But, since I write this text on my word processor, these variants will remain forever lost.)

I have augmented my archive, however, and this has resulted in a major change in my relation to this text I am producing. The change involves a kind of paradox. It has led me to a new conclusion, both textually and conceptually. That is to say, it has confirmed my previous conclusions. This is a conclusion which, reached now, amounts to a new conclusion, though it replicates my earlier thought; it is not the thought, but the confirmation of the thought.

This is the situation. Three more papers have arrived. One of these settles a small theological problem, for I now see that a text which I took on April 1 to be a finished piece was in fact only a sketch or long abstract. I read this new text and am moved by (as it were) the random cloud of its brilliant details.

It is a strange text. It talks about itself all the time and offers weird heterodox ideas: for example, that the principle of identity, for documents as well as for texts, is unreliable; and that reading can be an event occurring on multiple planes (we read words in a schedule of syntaxes, but also in a schedule of productions). At its "conclusion," between the last two pages of text, I find a copy of a letter inserted. It is directed to someone else and asks for help in bringing the (surrounding) text to a conclusion, or help in rewriting it altogether. I am not sure if this letter has found its way into my text "accidentally." I am not sure if the letter is "genuine" (it is dated April 1, 1985)! Is this letter a cri de coeur or an ironical gesture? Does it belong here? Of what "text" is it a part? And is this a "finished" document? In what sense? It is longer than its (apparent) "first version" seen by me several weeks ago, but is it therefore more *complete*?

WHAT DOES IT ALL MEAN?

I am reading one of my other new documents. I come upon the following words: "Instability is an essential feature of the text in process. Nevertheless, the author who is always free to continue to revise is also free by an act of will to close the process of revision." Is this, I wonder, an act of "free" will? My word processor tells me I am composing a ninth page of this present text, and I am imagining the circumstances when the text will be delivered—the time constraints, etc. Am I really free to continue this text, and free to close it when I like?

All of my new documents speak eloquently of the indeterminacy of texts, of their openness and their self-referencing structures. Texts are "free," and so are the makers of those texts.

But it seems to me, sometimes, that readers and editors may be seen as well, *even as they are readers and editors*, as authors and writers. And it also seems to me that authors and writers may be seen as well, *even as they are authors and writers*, as readers and editors. I am not "free" with respect to this text I am writing. Even as I write it I am reading it as if I were in another time and place—as if I were here and now, in fact—and my text, my "textualité," is constrained and determined by a future which at all points impinges upon my present text. This is to be in the textual condition.

I am in my room in the Royalton Hotel and it is 11 P.M. on April 25. I have to finish this text. But I read instead an interview in *The New Left Review*, where Gore Vidal observes the following: "We live in a literate world, but we live at another great hinge in history, when we are going beyond writing." This seems to me a shrewd assessment of our current involvements with textual instabilities. We are beginning to produce editions, and theories of editing, which illustrate what it means to be in the textual condition. Yet these editions themselves continually hint at an inevitable move "beyond writing," a move into a space of electronically mediated communication where "texts" adopt and require various kinds of simultaneous yet multiple engagements. The new edition of *Ulysses* is produced in a "literate" world, but in my judgment it has already moved us well "beyond writing."

This is not theory or interpretation; this is already fact. Two months ago a friend of mine—a well-known poet—sent me what appeared to be a book which bore his name on what appeared to be the title page. The dust jacket named this work *Mindwheel*, but no indication of authorship was to be found on that dust jacket. And on the title page, besides the name of my friend, Robert Pinsky, appeared the names of two other people—computer programmers. The book has a computer disc in a sleeve inside the back cover. Many of its pages are blank—they are to be filled in by the reader—while others have various types of odd texts. Some are narrative, but the "book" has many pictures, lists of instructions, indexes of relevant materials, and other odd paraphernalia. It is an electronic novel—the first ever published, I understand. It will not be the last.

This object looks like a book but can't really be called "a book." To say that one might "read" this "book" is to speak metaphorically. And then, what of its "authorship?" Or might one try to imagine the process of its "writing?"

In truth, this object is a bit of a freak, but like most monsters since Frankenstein's creation, it speaks unusual, disorienting truths for anyone who is interested in texts. It reminds me that although I still do "read" some books sometimes, most of my life is occupied with books in other ways entirely. Would anyone think that Hans Gabler's edition of *Ulysses* is a work to be *read*? I would remind you that Francis Bacon, three and a half centuries ago, may have had us in mind when he observed: "Some books are to be tasted, others to be swallowed, and some few to be chewed and digested." He said he was speaking metaphorically, but I am no longer so sure.

It is now Saturday, April 27, and the hour is 4:25 P.M. I have finally caught up with my text—or perhaps I should say that this text has finally caught up with itself. It has the sense of an ending at last.

But before it passes—like "virtuous men"—mildly away, I shall have to add two brief notes which reflect what I have learned since I last revised my paper just before dinner last night.

First, something on the matter of copy-text editing. If anyone attempts a critical edition based upon copy-text editing— I speak here primarily, though not exclusively, of nineteenth- and twentieth-century works—you must be prepared to find that the rule of final intentions may very well fail to provide an unambiguous guide to your decision. Sometimes the ambiguity results from a difficulty of fixing "authorial intention" within an extremely complex productive situation. "Author's intentions" enter into complicated relations with the productive activities of other persons, and the various lines of agency often become obscured. Sometimes, however, the ambiguity results from the difficulty of fixing precisely when the author "achieved" his or her "intentions." That happy moment is by no means clearly determinable. Indeed, it often changes in strange ways.

The second point I want to make involves a larger pedagogical and scholarly matter. It involves the question of the context in which all forms of scholarship are pursued and validated.

The separation of "scholarship" and "hermeneutics" (so-called) has been and continues to be encouraged. As I have argued elsewhere, this divorce in literary studies has seriously weakened literary-critical work along all its disciplinary lines. To date, most of my work in these two areas has been concentrated in attempts to persuade the "hermeneutics" that they cannot pursue their studies critically if they continue to operate in disregard of historical methods and the disciplines of positive knowledge. By the same token—and this is what *our* organization has to remember—specialized scholarly work, and in particular editorial and textual work, suffers a corresponding blindness when it is pursued in practical ignorance of its larger literary context. It is not wisdom to encourage or maintain the segregation of positive and hermeneutical discourse. To do so may appear to promote clarity and precision—may in fact at times do so—but it may, and does, equally promote a serious diminution in critical thinking, properly so called.

It is an illusion of scholars to think that whereas a special privilege—the possibility of rigor and precision—lies within the range of textual and bibliocritical discourse, it stands beyond the reach of hermeneutics, which is a house built of sand. This illusion is based on various misconceptions, the most prevalent of which holds that so-called positive knowledge, factual information, and documentary materials provide the basic ground of stability in critical thinking. The truth is in fact far more difficult and elusive. The truth is that all forms and states of knowledge, including factual and documentary knowledge, are mediated in precise and determinate ways. These mediations introduce determinate—and hence critically specifiable—instabilities into every kind of investigation. Scholarship is interpretation, whether it is carried out as a bibliocritical discourse or a literary exegesis. Though we scholars like to believe that one is prior to the other—though we are told, for example, by René Wellek that textual studies are "preliminary operations" to interpretive work—this idea is at best a specialized hypothesis for programmatic work, and at worst a deep critical illusion.

It is an idea to which we, as members of this organization, are especially liable. To accept it is bad for literary studies as a whole. For *us* to accept it, moreover, is especially unfortunate, since this is the organization, and we are the people, in possession of the technical skills which offer some hope for bringing about an end to the schism in literary studies.

I think now—at 4:30 P.M. today—that my text and my meaning have at last come together, for the time being at any rate.

PART TWO

Ezra Pound in the Sixth Chamber

We do not exist in the majority of these times; in some you exist, and not I; in others I, and not you; in others, both of us. In the present one, which a favorable fate has granted me, you have arrived at my house; in another, while crossing the garden, you found me dead; in still another, I utter these same words, but I am a mistake, a ghost.

—Jorge Luis Borges, *"The Garden of Forking Paths"*

The demand for an adequate mode of expression is senseless.

—Kathy Acker, *Empire of the Senseless*

5

How to Read a Book

FOR EIGHT YEARS millions of people could scarcely avoid repeated contact with the following text.

It came to us as a narrativized series of sounds and images on the television screen. In the background is the White House (or Camp David, or a ranch in California). In the middle distance is a large helicopter, its rotors sending out their characteristic chuffing noises. The decibels are running fairly high. Then the camera picks up Ronald and Nancy Reagan, often with their dog in leash-tow, moving diagonally across the screen from the background building to the waiting helicopter. Both are smiling and waving toward the television camera, which serves as the surrogate of ourselves, the watchers.

At the corners of this camera's eye can be seen a group of agitated journalists. As soon as the Reagans and their dog emerge from the building and come into the field dominated by the helicopter and its noise, the journalists begin hurling questions. The questions, like the obedient children of legend, can be seen but not heard—or not heard distinctly—by us the watchers, or (evidently) by Ronald Reagan, who continues to smile as he cups his ear, appearing to try to make out what he is being asked. He will shrug his shoulders—alas, the noise is just too great, the questioned cannot hear the questioners. Besides, in another four or five steps he will enter the waiting helicopter (the Reagans and their dog, after emerging from the house, have not paused in their stroll).

I could go on describing further details of this fascinating scene: for instance, the image of the journalists growing increasingly frantic in their questions as the Reagans near the entrance hole of the helicopter; the correspondent (and contrastive) image of the security people, who exhibit perfect self-control, appearing to care only for their (selfless) task of looking after the welfare of the president, oblivious to the turmoil in which the journalists are involved; that slick final moment when the Reagans reach the steps to the helicopter and turn to make their last ceremonial waves and smiles, the moment when the journalists take the cue and fall silent—it is too late for questions now; now there is time only for the ritual farewell to and by the ritual head of state.

The most important persons in this text are invisible. They are ourselves, the unseen presences for whom the display has principally been constructed. The scenic narrative is a classic example of what is meant by propaganda—in this case, the manipulation of the social institution of the so-called free press for certain state political purposes. This is not a "news event"; it is the illusion of a news event, a ceremony of the news.

Many people are aware of this, of course, and while the scene has been critically commented upon before, no one, so far as I know, has pointed out the following extraordinary fact: that in a scene where speaking and communicating with words appear to be of central importance, language has been structurally translated into visual and oral tokens—as image, or as nonlinguistic sound. Complex meanings are being communicated here, but the verbal discourse—Pound's "logopoeia"—functions principally along nonverbal lines. To understand this text it is not necessary actually to hear anything said by Reagan or anything asked by the reporters.

This is the form of what I suppose we should now have to call "great communication"—to be named as such after its principal vehicle, the Great Communicator, who employed it—or rather, who was employed by it—between 1980 and 1988.

But of course this is a "media text"—not a book, and least of all a poem. Reading a book is very different from reading a television screen. And we all should certainly agree that great differences are involved here. Nonetheless, "Reagan's Farewell" (for such is the title I shall give to this text, Reagan's best performance in a short-subject film) exhibits a textual structure which can help us understand how books and even poems communicate—just as the latter can help us, reciprocally, to understand the character of a text like "Reagan's Farewell."

I will begin to explore these matters by posing this question: What is the structure of the act of reading? The question has fascinated Americans, and especially American educators, throughout this century. Mortimer Adler's *How to Read a Book: The Art of Getting a Liberal Education* (1940) was one of the most famous and influential of a whole series of similar books, pamphlets, and textbooks designed to teach the "art" of reading. Almost equally famous and (finally even more) influential was Ezra Pound's *ABC of Reading*, first published in 1934. Adler's book has been out of print for some time; Pound's book is still available from New Directions, and is even taught in some schools (though usually as part of specialized courses in twentieth-century literature or culture).

Unlike Adler's book, *ABC of Reading* is aggressively anti-academic. Nevertheless, it shares with Adler's book the view that "the fate of reading" (as it were) is the Great Book (so-called). Learning "how to read a book" means putting oneself to school to those who know how to read and—even more important—who know what are the important books to read. Reading has to be grounded in the Great Books because they alone can provide stable models of excellence—standards by which to measure other texts, both good and bad. In this sense, *How to Read a Book* and *ABC of Reading* are both about how to read a *great* book (or text). In each case active readers are postulated who will put themselves to school to the best that has been known and thought in the world.

In Adler's and Pound's books—they are quite typical of the genre—"reading" is equated with deciphering the linguistic text. This equation is most clearly maintained in Adler's book, which is academically grounded. For Adler, "how to read a book" means learning how to decode "one kind of readable symbol, the kind which men invent for the purpose of communication—the words of human language."[1] To read is to acquire possession of the text's *verbum*, its *logos*, its conceptual content. Adler's model of reading is ultimately a hermeneutic (as opposed to a constructivist) one: in a seventeenth- or eighteenth-century battle of the books, Adler would come down on the side of the ancients rather than the moderns.[2]

Although Pound's book, at its expository level, makes many of the same assumptions about the act of reading, its structure and format suggest very different commitments. *ABC of Reading* has engaged in the battle of the books, but finally it has not been able to make up its mind whether reading is an act of decoding or an act of construction. *ABC of Reading* is at least as much a text about writing as it is about reading.

The differences between Adler's book and Pound's are nicely displayed at the most physical and apparitional levels. Adler's book is twice as long as Pound's, and while both are published by established houses (Simon and Schuster, in Adler's case; Faber and Faber, and Yale University Press, in Pound's), Adler's book is a much more sober performance. Half of Pound's book is comprised of reading exercises and exhibits, while Adler's—by contrast—is a four-hundred page tome written in a style that is at once clear, ponderous, and inexorable. For all its title of "How to," Adler's book resembles a series of academic lectures.

Pound's text, on the other hand, does resemble a "how to" book. This feature is quite apparent in its long series of "Exhibits," which Pound uses as practical illustrations of certain kinds of writing. But it is also foregrounded in a dramatic way by the book's formatting. *ABC of Reading* uses capitals, boldface, and italics to emphasize one point or another—like advertising texts, public notices, broadsides, or (the descendents of such texts) like a modernist manifesto. Furthermore, the parts of the book—sentences, paragraphs, sections—are strategically arranged to draw the reader's eye into the book: to involve the reader's visual encounter with the text, in the arguments which the text is making.

These physical aspects of Pound's book carry out his expository argument at the work's illustrative level. Pound is, like Adler, committed to the tradition of the Great Book, but his engagement with that tradition is largely constructivist and modern (rather than hermeneutic and neoclassical/romantic). For example, chapter 6 begins like this:

For *those who read only English*, I have done what I can.

I have translated the TA HIO so that they can learn where to start THINKING. And I have translated the Seafarer; so that they can see more or less where English poetry starts. . . .

You can get Ovid, or rather Ovid's stories, in Golding's "Metamorphoses," which is the most beautiful book in the language (my opinion and I suspect it was Shakespeare's).

Marlowe translated the "Amores."

And before that Gavin Douglas had made something of the Aeneids that I, at any rate, like better than Virgil's Latin.[3]

The physical presentation of pages like this is simultaneously a display of their conceptual content. The use of italics, capitals, and paragraphing are the signs of their constructivist orientation. Pound's Gavin Douglas—who made a translation that is being judged, in Pound's text, "better than Virgil's Latin"—is a *figura* of that constructivism. Pound's Great Books, it turns out, comprise an archive of great originals and great reconstructions—the latter often rivalling and even surpassing their forebears. Pound is himself the master of these ceremonies of reconstruction.

I I

In this general context, then, let me ask once more the question: "What is the structure of the act of reading?" Like Adler, we commonly think this question will be addressed by analyzing the linear processes of the linguistic text. That is to say, we seek to investigate that form of reading by which one moves from grapheme to word to phrase to sentence and, thence, on through the larger rhetorical and generic forms which make up the linguistic text. Once again Pound's *ABC of Reading* is a most useful point of departure because Pound's theory of writing and reading is caught in a conflict of commitments. The conflict is clear in the following famous passage from chapter 4:

> The charging of language is done in three principal ways: . . . called phanopoeia, melopoeia, logopoeia. You use a word to throw a visual image on to the reader's imagination, or you charge it by sound, or you use groups of words to do this.
> Thirdly, you take the greater risk of using the word in some special relation to "usage," that is, to the kind of context in which the reader expects, or is accustomed, to find it.[4]

In this formulation Pound remains tied to a linguistic model of language. His linguistic orientation is most apparent in his definition of phanopoeia, which evidently does not correspond to his own practice as a writer. For in Pound's work, phanopoeia may be observed not only in "images" evoked by words and strings of words; it operates as well as rhetorical and even abstract constructions of the page as a visual field.

We have already seen Pound employ constructivist procedures even in *ABC of Reading*, but the method is most elaborately deployed in the *Cantos*, which use decorative materials
in ways that distinctly (and deliberately) recall the tradition
of ornamental books passed on to Pound by William Morris
and the late nineteenth century in general (for an example see
figure 8 in chapter 6). Because Pound is "quoting" those traditions, however, the illustrative materials function at an abstract and cognitive level at least as much as they do at an
imagistic level. Though grounded in the tradition of symbolic
book illustration, this kind of page is highly abstract and self-
referential, and distinctly anticipates the presentational forms
developed by action painting and that movement's more rep-
resentational (postmodern) inheritors.[5]

The second example, from Canto LXXXVI, underscores
the point. Much has been made of Pound's ideogrammic
theories, and the view persists—through some of Pound's
own misleading (and contradicted) misconceptions—that the
ideogram is for Pound a kind of image. On the contrary, the
ideogram is for Pound the *idea of the image*. In the *Cantos*,
therefore, Chinese ideograms function not linguistically or
logically but *phenomenologically*, like the abstract and conceptual forms in action paintings. On page 567 from Canto
LXXXVI, for example, the ideograms are carefully arranged
on the field of the page as a kind of "unwobbling pivot" for
the more nervous play of the European text[6] (see illus. 3).
Phanopoeia, melopoeia, and logopoeia become, as a consequence, completely interinvolved, and the page emerges as
what Roy Wagner has called a symbol that stands for itself.[7]

This concept of the self-standing symbol is all but explicit
in Pound's theory of the ideogram. The Chung character,
which means (approximately) "center" or "balance," is
Pound's *figura* of the unwobbling pivot—for reasons that are
clear enough if we simply look at one or another of the appearances of that character in the *Cantos*—for example, illus-

tration 4 from page 464. Pound, however, generalizes his theory of the ideogram in the *Cantos* by making all the Chinese characters function as *figurae* of stability in relation to the sequential and temporalized orders of Western language syntaxes.

So, in reading page 567 from Canto LXXXVI we may take the ordered line of Chinese ideograms as a phanopoeic allusion to Pound's idea of the unwobbling pivot. The page may, in this respect, "throw a visual image [of the unwobbling pivot] on to the reader's imagination." But the page need not be taken that way; it may also be read as a gestalt for organizing the way the eye will scan the page and its heteronomous characters. The latter is its principal—that is to say, its rhetorical—function. This function is perhaps even more clearly shown on page 566, where the different sizes of the ideograms correspond to the rhetorical use of typography which we saw earlier in *ABC of Reading* (see illus. 5).

The abstract and conceptual aspect of the melopoeia of these texts can be observed by paying attention to another feature of Pound's presentation of his Chinese material (pages 544–45) (see illus. 6). Pound's text supplies the ideograms with their oral equivalents, but it does this conceptually—as the numerical superscripts indicate. These numbers are the conventional signs by which linguists indicate the tonal values to be given to the different phonetic equivalents of the ideographic characters. The tones are crucial because in Chinese the same "word" will "mean" completely different things, depending upon the tone of the utterance.

This last example shows very plainly, therefore, how the linguistic and linear reading model may not by any means comprehend the structure within which the reading process is to be executed. At least two other structures operate in every act of reading. The first of these—spatial reading—is repeatedly called out by the *Cantos* and even *ABC of Reading*; but it is a ubiquitous function of texts, although some dramatize its demands more than others.

Iou Wang, 770

King Jou

killed by barbarians

"I

Houo

in angustiis me defendisti,
"Millet wine, fragrant,
and a red bow
with a hundred arrows
and a black bow
and a hundred arrows.
ne inutile quiescas."   end quote.
"Will not rustle cattle,
will not take oxen and horses,
will close all traps and pitfalls
that they have set for wild game"

Pe

K'in

order for mobilization against insurrection
by tribes from t'other side of the Houai river

567

3. Ezra Pound, *Cantos*: New Directions edition,
tenth printing, p. 567.

LXXVII

AND this day Abner lifted a shovel. . . . .
                instead of watchin' it to see if it would
        take action

Von Tirpitz said to his daughter..as we have elsewhere
recorded / he said: beware of their charm
                But on the other hand Maukch thought he
would do me a favour by getting me onto the commission
to inspect the mass graves at Katin,
                le beau monde gouverne
        if not toujours at any rate it is a level of
some sort whereto things tend to return
                Chung

                in the middle 中

whether upright or horizontal
        " and having got 'em (advantages, privilege)
there is nothing, italics *nothing*, they will not do
to retain 'em "
                yrs truly   Kungfutseu
Entered the Bros Watson's store in Clinton N. Y.
        preceded by a crash, i.e. by a
huge gripsack or satchel
which fell and skidded along the 20 foot aisle-way
and ceased with a rumpus of glassware
        (unbreakable as it proved)
        and with the enquiry: WOT IZZA COMIN'?

" I'll tell you wot izza comin'
                Sochy-lism is a-comin'

464

4. Ezra Pound, *Cantos*: New Directions edition, tenth
        printing, p. 464.

Up out of Tuscany, Leopoldine.
"We don't hate anybody."
                              Quoted Konody,
"We fight when our Emperor says so."
                      (Austrians 1914)
"Decent chaps" (Schwartz '43)
            "a shame that we have to fight 'em."
"Mais le prussien!
            Le prussien
                      c'est un chic homme."
Said the aged femme de ménage with four teeth out.
      "Vous voullez me rouler,
            mais 'ous ne me
                      roulerez pas,
"paaasque je suis trop rosse."

litigantium dona   féi

                                         pào

non coelum non in medio
            but man is under Fortuna
? that is a forced translation?
            La donna che volgo
Man under Fortune,

            CHÊN

566

5. Ezra Pound, *Cantos*: New Directions edition,
       tenth printing, p. 566.

THE FOUR TUAN'

端 shih²

時

忐 ch'ên²

or foundations.

Hulled rice and silk at easter
    (with the *bachi* held under their aprons
From T'ang's time until now)
That you lean 'gainst the tree of heaven,
    and know Ygdrasail

poi

"Birds and terrapin lived under Hia,
    beast and fish held their order,
Neither flood nor flame falling in excess"
                                            i
                                         moua
                                          pou
                                         gning

Perspicax qui excolit se ipsum,
Their writings wither because they have no curiosity,
This "leader", gouged pumpkin
    that they hoist on a pole,

and jump to the winning side
                        (urbae)
                        tchõung

II. 9. have scopes and beginnings
                        chèu

仁 智   chih⁴   i-li
jen²
are called chung¹·⁴

衷

仁 好   (1508, Mathews)

甲

no mere epitome without organization.
        The sun under it all:
    Justice, d'urbanité, de prudence

wei heou,   Σοφία

the sheltered grass hopes, chueh, chueh, cohere.
    (No, that is *not* philological)
Not led of lusting, not of contriving
    but is as the grass and tree

eccellenza

    not led of lusting,
    not of the worm, contriving

6. Ezra Pound, *Cantos*: New Directions edition, tenth printing, pp. 544–45.

To read Blake's illuminated poems, or any newspaper, is to be reminded of the crucial importance which spatial relations play in the structure of texts. Texts printed in a newspaper have a spatial structure very different from texts printed in a book, or even in a magazine. The differences are important because they involve semiotic codes which readers will decipher—more or less fully, and whether consciously or not. Such differences are clear to us if, for example, we think of reading a text (say a poem) in a typescript or a manuscript, and reading the same text in a printed and published format. The physical space occupied by the text is, in each case, very different and calls out correspondingly different modes of reading.

The reading eye does not move only in a linear direction. Blake's works are particularly useful for reminding us that the reading eye is a scanning mechanism as well as a linear decoder. We are familiar with Mallarmé's *Un Coup de Des* and Apollinaire's *Calligrammes*, and the spatial deployments of the page carried out by many other modern poets.[8] These texts are not so different from ideographic works like Herbert's "The Altar." But all poetry, even in its most traditional forms, asks the reader to decipher the text in spatial as well as linear terms. Stanzaic and generic forms, rhyme schemes, metrical orders: all of these deploy spatial functions in scripted texts, as their own roots in oral poetry's "visual" arts of memory should remind us. Even the prose poem communicates through its spatial arrangement. When the prose poem artfully reintroduces a purely linear appearance into the text, it paradoxically heightens our sense of the spatial form of the work. Consciously or not, readers of prose poems recognize and decode that spatiality.

When Yeats reprinted, in his *Oxford Book of Modern Verse 1892–1935* (1936), Pater's famous description of the *Mona Lisa*, he graphically demonstrated the semiotic power of the spatial arrangement of a text. Yeats printed the original prose passage as a piece of free verse. In doing this he was implicitly offering a theory of the prose poem (it is by no means the only possible theory). Yeats's theory is a symbolist one, and it contrasts sharply with the more recent constructivist theory elaborated by Ron Silliman.[9]

In addition, however, he was making an argument about the literary history of modernism itself. Yeats did not elaborate his argument in expository detail, however. He used the format and organization of the anthology to make his argument—literally, to cast his argument into a physical shape appropriate to his thought. The title of his book defined the schematic boundaries of Yeats's history (the title carried as a tailpiece the dates 1892–1935), but the placement of the famous text from Pater was a move to bring Yeats's theory of modernism into sharp and concrete focus. Yeats put the free verse Mona Lisa text at the very beginning of his edition (which signifies, bibliographically, "1892"),[10] and in so doing he used the format of his anthology to shape a complex historical argument about the origins of modernism. Crucial to the decipherment of Yeats's argument is a reading of the spatial text—a reading of the text's linear arrangement, on one hand, and its position in the book as a whole on the other.

This last point—the position of Yeats's Mona Lisa text within his book—draws our attention to another important spatial form which the reading eye decodes. Reading much contemporary work on texts one might easily overlook the relevance of these kinds of materiality.[11] Poems and literary texts provide many good instances of the way texts call out spatial modes of reading in their audiences. But all texts do the same, only some operate more clearly than others. One thinks, for example, of advertising texts, which typically are collaged assemblies of different kinds of scripted materials, including many different type fonts and sizes. Advertising texts, like poems, insist that their audiences manipulate both linear and spatial modes of reading. Two great styles have dominated the spatial form of such texts—the "soft" and the "hard"—and both are instantly recognizable: one advertises a Mercedes Benz or a BMW with a "soft" text, whereas "hard" texts are typically used to market the cheaper lines of cars.

These two spatial styles (or codes) appear in a wide range of variant types. We do not have to read a single word of many newspaper texts in order to have already "read" part of what they are saying. Material printed in *The New York Times* will necessarily be read very differently from material printed in, for example, *USA Today*. Both represent themselves as national newspapers, but the formatting of these two dailies is radically different, and the difference calls out to very different reading expectations and procedures. News magazines like *Time* and *Newsweek* organize their materials—including their advertisements—with great care, and the formatting arrangements design specific kinds of reading processes (which we can either follow, or *choose to* resist—or, after that choice has become possible, which we can once again *choose to* follow). In the same way, the very physique of a book will embody a code of meaning which the reader will decipher, more or less deeply, more or less self-consciously. To read, for example, a translation of Homer's *Iliad* in the Signet paperback, in the edition published by the University of Chicago Press, in the Norton Critical Edition, or in the limited edition put out by the Folio Society (with illustrations), is to read Homer's *Iliad* in four very different ways. Each of these texts is visually and materially coded for different audiences and different purposes.

The way that advertising skills are taught in art school is significant and illuminating. Every advertising text is theorized in two parts, the graphic and the linguistic—the one under the authority of the art director, the other of the copywriter. The two can be one person, of course, and in the final

115

product the two functions must be coordinated. But in art school the student is first taught to treat the entire work graphically, not linguistically. This fact appears in the convention which governs the handling of advertising copy in student advertising exercises. The linguistic text, which the student buys at an art supply store (!), comprises a parodic kind of fractured Latin—blocks of linguistic nonsense organized into word strings, sentences, and paragraphs.

In this textual imagination the "reading eye" is taken to be primarily (if not purely) ocular, as if the "reading eye" and the physical organs of sight could be, but do not *have* to be, distinguished. But there is a third kind of reading—what I have elsewhere called "radial reading"—in which the activity of reading regularly transcends its own ocular physical bases.[12] When Pound speaks of using words "in some special relation to 'usage',", he had this form of reading in mind. The elementary sign of radial reading is probably illustrated by a person who rises from reading a book in order to look up the meaning of a word in a dictionary or to check some historical or geographical reference.

So much has been made of Pound's ideas about logopoeia, melopoeia, and phanopoeia that most have neglected what he had to say about "usage," and the importance (therefore) of the *Cantos'* use of dialectal forms (in several languages) and of quoted materials. Since Pound is not the exclusive focus of this discussion, however, I raise the matter simply to call attention to the larger functions which Pound was imagining for his materialist textual innovations. Toward the end of the Pisan Cantos—in fact, at the penultimate page of Canto LXXXIV in the New Directions collected *Cantos*—we confront the following text (page 539) (see illus. 7). I am interested only in the last two lines of this text, where the Chinese "word" $Ming^2$ appears in the English text that reads, "These are distinctions in clarity/ $Ming^2$ [ideogram] these are distinctions."[13]

116

and my old great aunt did likewise
with that too large hotel
but at least she saw damn all Europe
    and rode on that mule in Tangiers
        and in general had a run for her money

like Natalie
      " perhaps more than was in it "

    Under white clouds, cielo di Pisa
out of all this beauty something must come,

O moon my pin-up,
          chronometer
Wei, Chi and Pi-kan
Yin had these three men full of humanitas (manhood)
        or jên[2]
Xaire Alessandro
        Xaire Fernando, e il Capo,
Pierre, Vidkun,
      Henriot
and as to gradations
who went out of industrials into Government
    when the slump was in the offing
as against whom, prepense, got OUT of Imperial Chemicals
in 1938
so as not to be nourished by blood-bath?

quand vos venetz al som de l'escalina
         ἦθος gradations
These are distinctions in clarity

ming[2] 明   these are distinctions

539

7. Ezra Pound, *Cantos*: New Directions edition,
tenth printing, p. 539.

This text is an enactment of the ideas it is concerned with, ideas about clarity, making distinctions, and ultimately about the need for paying attention. The superscript "2" might have been 1, 2, 3, or 4—it draws a melopoeic distinction which has to be attended to if we are to "read" the text. The ideogram itself is comprised of a pair of independent characters, the first being the character phonologically rendered "Jih," and meaning "sun," the second the character phonologically "Yeuh," meaning "moon." This new Ming^2 character, by collocating the two, draws us to see that Ming^2 is (literally) a distinctive character—a character whose "meaning" derives from the evident similarities and differences between its two component parts. In the composite character the two are brought together as a single *figura* which literally means something like "the fall of light" (a key Poundian image). By extension the ideogram signifies "intelligence," and this more abstract meaning is (as it were) dramatized in the ideogram itself, where the two base characters are joined but also distinguished.

I shall not extend my commentary beyond this general observation: that Pound's highly spatialized text may—indeed, must—also be read as a double injunction. In the first place, the reader is called to pay the closest attention to every detail of the passage. In the second, readers are enjoined to see that "reading" is not a natural but an acquired skill, a skill deeply imbedded in distinct societies and distinct histories. For a Western reader, this text will have to be put down for a time, and returned to later, if it is to be read.

And note the implication of this injunction. Because one must consciously acquire the ability to read the Chinese material in the text, the passage tells us something about the English text as well—a part of the text which we native readers (Pound's immediate audience) tend to forget: that there is no such thing as a "natural language." All language is a constructive acquisition, and to the degree that we treat it as a "natural" phenomenon, to that degree we have abandoned the possibility of exercising control over it. For readers this means that the texts will control us, and not we them.

But I take it as axiomatic that reading, like writing and speaking, is a type of communicative exchange, and hence works through a structure of reciprocals. Consequently, the last example of a Poundian spatialized text points us in the direction of what Pound called "usage." The spatial text already has a radial inertia which no reader will find it easy to avoid.

Radial reading involves decoding one or more of the contexts that interpenetrate the scripted and physical text. It necessitates some kind of abstraction from what appears most immediately. The person who temporarily stops "reading" to look up the meaning of a word is properly an *emblem* of radial reading because that kind of "radial" operation is repeatedly taking place even while one remains absorbed with a text. Emily Dickinson tells us that "there is no frigate like a book" in order to remind us that reading sends us away from, and with, the books we enter.

Some texts foreground and encourage acts of radial reading, whereas others work to prevent or limit radial processing. A good instance of the latter would be a Harlequin romance or a bodice ripper or some similar kind of text. In these cases the text tries to establish a reading field that is as completely self-absorbed as possible, so that the reader does not have to reflect upon the scene of reading at all. Of course such works *can* and should be read critically, and in the scholarship of popular culture we observe good readers brushing such texts against their own grain in order to deconstruct the meanings they work to transmit. But works like these do not positively call out to the critical and self-conscious reader—on the contrary, in fact.

In this respect, the Harlequin romance stands in the sharpest contrast to critical texts of various kinds, where radial readings in the scripted forms are encouraged. What is called "scholarship" is one territory—highly specialized to be sure—where radial types of reading are continually being put into practice. To the extent that the work of scholarship is an intramural set of operations, we would have to see its radial readings as essentially technological rather than critical. Nevertheless, because scholarly texts are works which can only be read consciously and with great deliberateness, they provide a number of excellent examples of texts which encourage radial reading.

Perhaps the most striking example of such a text is the so-called critical edition—for instance, the Cornell Wordsworth volumes, or any of the editions of English authors produced through the Oxford English Texts series. One does not simply move through works like these in a linear way, starting at the beginning and then proceeding page by sequential page. Rather, one moves around the edition, jumping from the reading text to the apparatus, perhaps from one of these to the notes or to an appendix, perhaps then back to some part of the front matter which may be relevant, and so forth. The edition also typically drives one to other books and acts of reading, ancillary or related materials which have to be drawn into the reading process in order to expand and enrich the textual and the reading field.

This is a process by which the entire sociohistory of the work—from its originary moments of production through all its subsequent reproductive adventures—is postulated as the ultimate goal of critical self-consciousness. That the goal is in fact an unreachable one is clear. A practical move toward its attainment is essential to criticism, however. Such a move appears as some particular version of a work—say, Hyder Rollins's Variorum edition of Shakespeare's Sonnets, or Stephen Booth's more recent critical edition. Each is a particular attempt to define a comprehensive sociohistorical field for the sonnets. Whereas Rollins works with a traditional apparatus,

Booth's edition is framed as a set of facing-page texts which dramatize the historical gap separating us from early seventeenth-century readers. The particular significance of these two editions is as much a function of their limits as of their special strengths, both of which they execute as corresponding sets of presences and absences.

In this respect the critical edition is a kind of analogue computer designed to reconstitute past texts and versions in forms which make them usable in the present and for the future.[14] The special hermeneutic advantage of such an edition over, say, a more simple "reading edition" lies in its theoretical comprehensiveness: the complexity of the critical edition allows one to imagine many possible states of the text, including various types of "reading" and "student" and "modernized" editions. Noncritical editions are much more limited in this respect.

Critical editions take many forms, of course, and some are better—are more accurate or more complex—than others. Nor can that computer we might call the critical edition be programmed to regenerate anything but analogues of the texts in which it is interested. This is one of its key structural limitations; the other is the selection processes which will be built into its programs. Still, the example of the critical edition is useful for clarifying the theory of texts because it is, to this point in time, one of the most sociohistorically self-conscious of texts. Because it also emphasizes, *in itself*, the constructed and agented character of a text, it has the additional advantage of opening itself to critical reading, and thence of breaking down that spell of self-transparency which hovers over all the texts we read.

When we teach reading in our classrooms, we typically stand to our students in much the same relation that the critical edition stands to us when we read (for example) *Ulysses*. That is to say, we try to structure the reading field in order to encourage students to free themselves from the tyranny of the immediate and the linear text. Good readers have to read both linearly and spatially, but both of those operations remain closely tied to the illusion of textual immediacy. Radial reading is the most advanced, the most difficult, and the most important form of reading because radial reading alone puts one in a position to respond actively to the text's own (often secret) discursive acts.

Let me begin to illustrate this point by recalling two of my earlier examples. The reading of the Yeats *Oxford Book of Modern Verse*, and, in particular, of its opening Pater text, acquires point and depth only when it involves a simultaneous rereading of the original passage from *The Renaissance*; and this dialectical act of reading constitutes a textual translation that far transcends either of the two Paterian texts, or both together. It involves, that is, a reading of a particular act of writing coded, but by no means fully visibilized, in Yeats's book—which is a radial text with many complex filiations that reach out across space and time.

This example from Yeats may remind us how radial reading operates as a function of linear and spatial reading. One sees the same connection in the two volumes which comprise the first editions of Pound's first twenty-seven cantos. Each of those books makes a clear historical allusion not only to William Morris and the bibliographical face of the late nineteenth-century aesthetic movement, but also to the longer tradition which those late nineteenth-century works were invoking: the tradition of the decorated manuscript and its Renaissance bibliographical inheritors.[15] The linear and spatial codes of such a text function properly only within the horizon of radial reading which the book has invoked.

But that radial field is by no means the only one in which Pound's book is involved. Once again, we are cued to the presence of this other field by certain material features of *A Draft of XVI. Cantos*. The title page states that the decorative material in the book was done by the artist Henry

Strater; there is an imprint on page [67] stating that the book was produced at Three Mountains Press in Paris, over a fairly extensive period of time (May–December 1924); and a colophon on page [2] declares: "The Edition of Ninety Copies consists of Five on Imperial Japan paper autographed by the author lettered A to E Fifteen on Whatman paper numbered I to XV and Seventy on Roma paper specially watermarked numbered 1 to 70." *A Draft of XVI. Cantos*, in other words, is a collaborative project, as all books are. Its collaborations are also of a very specific and determinable kind which Pound's poetical text not only summons but finally must submit to as well. The title page, imprint, and colophon have to be carefully *read* if we want to be clear about the context within which Pound's poem was being initially defined. Not least important, in this connection, is the circle of readers which the book embraces. Equally significant are the historical allusions being made through the use of the conventions of "fine printing" in the late nineteenth and early twentieth century. When one reads the book titled *A Draft of XVI. Cantos*, the purely linguistic text is imbedded in a radial network one can hardly fail to register; so physically, so dramatically has that network been presented at the level of the book's bibliographical codes.

With the passage of time new communicative circumstances develop—new editions are produced—which turn the text into a kind of palimpsest. The work called the *Cantos* which descends to us incorporates, however invisibly, all of its accumulated history, and this history includes a book like *A Draft of XVI. Cantos* (as the latter had included, *self-consciously*, the entire history of book production). To read the *Cantos* today is therefore necessarily to encounter all the earlier incarnations of the descended text in a translated form. Reconstituting the presence of an ancestral text like *A Draft of XVI. Cantos* is a highly specialized and self-conscious type of reading, but it is a fundamental and necessary exercise—indeed, it seems to me the model for every act of reading, even a reading which appears to be situated only and wholly in the present. To read *A Draft of XVI. Cantos*, in face of the standard New Directions collected *Cantos*, is to explode the self-transparency of the latter as a mere apparition. It is to be placed in a position of reading readiness— alive to the fact that the text is and has always been involved in complex radial networks and communicative exchanges.

From the producers' point of view, every book—indeed, every scripted text—is a code of signals designed to put specific sets of such interchanges in operation. Readers, for their part, decode the signals, but that is not all they do. They also retransmit, functioning as secondary authorities who interact with other readers, but who also re-act on the initial code of signals, complicating and altering the original messages.

In this very essay I am myself retransmitting Pound's work. Here is a brief reflexive narrative of one new line of "meaning" I am trying to set in motion:

"In 1925 Pound and his coproducers of *A Draft of XVI. Cantos* wanted to display their positive relation to late nineteenth-century poetic traditions. With the development of the ideology of modernism, however, the *Cantos* came to be read as the prototype of the twentieth century's reaction against and critique of Victorian poetry, and of the aesthetic movement in particular. Pound himself, a key ideologue of modernism, did much to foster such a reading of literary history. A radial encounter with the *Cantos*, however, exposes the differential reading options which Pound's work embodies—exposes, in short, the *contradictory* aims of his own project."

That "reading" is a reaction upon a textual field that comprises far more than the linguistic text, far more even than the linguistic and the spatial text. It is a reading which assumes that the physical texts of Pound's work are not only linguistic and spatial, but multiple and interactive as well. It is a reading which seeks to visibilize the textual field—the scene of radial reading—by a close observation of the materials, the means, and the modes of textual production as they develop and interact over time.

As the last example from Pound suggests, radial reading is a function of the historicity of texts. We observe its demands in the scene of a work's reception history, and throughout the stages of its reproductive development. John Sutherland's acute studies of the differing institutional forms by which the best seller is produced in England and in America expose one fundamental scene of radial reading.[16] Sutherland details, on one hand, the "English" model of postpublication reading via the traditional reviewing institutions; and, on the other, the "American" model of prepublication reading via early promotional apparatuses, advance printing and purchase orders, and various peripheral schemes for disseminating (not necessarily the text but) the presence of the the text. In each case, a great deal of important reading goes on which will not involve any direct encounter with the so-called text itself.

Sutherland sees the prepublication structures of reading as peculiarly American; and while it is true that American trade publishers refined and professionalized this kind of reading, they learned it from the English. Byron's first installment of *Childe Harold* in 1812 was a best seller, but its success had not been anticipated by prepublication readings. The first English poetical work to use the prepublication scene of reading in an important way was, appropriately enough, Tennyson's *In Memoriam* (1850). Twenty years later Dante Gabriel Rossetti's *Poems* (1870) was produced in an even more consciously (if not more successfully) defined process of prepublication moves and readings.

The most celebrated English poem of the twentieth century, *The Waste Land*, descends to us through a similar reception history. The famous story of its all but collaborative composition history, with Pound's urgent and sympathetic critical mind driving Eliot to reimagine and complete the poem, is only one facet of a much more elaborate and important story. When the poem was finally published in book form in December, 1922, its artistic importance had already been institutionally imagined, if not actually and finally decided.

The story, now being retold in fascinating detail by Lawrence Rainey, involves a complex act of reading (and writing) *The Waste Land* by various social agents and agencies in 1922.[17] I shall not rehearse the story here, but I will call attention to a few salient details. *The Waste Land* was first published in *The Dial* in November, 1922 in a complicated financial arrangement between *The Dial* people, Eliot, and the publishers Boni and Liveright, who had contracted to publish the poem in book form a few weeks after *The Dial* publication. The terms included giving Eliot the Dial Award for the year 1922 *as part of his publishing contract* with both of the publishers. When the poem appeared, in other words, it already wore the insignia of its special status and importance. Many of the early reviews are written in full consciousness of the import of those insignia. Their knowledge is perhaps most apparent in certain hostile reviews, which registered their disapproval at the special privileges which the poem had acquired for itself.

The first readers of Eliot's published poem encountered the work in a radial reading field that had already been sharply, if not wholly, defined. That horizon of reading would dominate *The Waste Land*'s reception history—the legend of the poem—for the rest of the century. To retell the story in all of its details is to step outside the circle of that initial horizon, and hence to reread *The Waste Land* with a clearer understanding of why it is a radial, and not simply a linguistic, text.

I I I

To see that books function in a radial field, that they interact with their contexts, carries important consequences for the way we will read them. For one thing, it forces us to realize that books involve a "reading" of their audiences which those audiences may or may not realize, and may or may not submit to. "Reagan's Farewell" means to interact with its audiences by absorbing and regularizing the possible modes of response. Unlike *The Waste Land*, it labors to minimize its own internal conflicts, as well as the possible conflicts its message might generate. In order for us to *read* "Reagan's Farewell," then, rather than simply be *read by* it, we have to explode the illusion of contextual seamlessness which the work projects. We have to "step outside" that fiction of a homogeneous context and read the work in a framework and point of view which it has not already absorbed and anticipated. This requires reading the work in those contexts which "Reagan's Farewell" has tried either to forbid, or to declare nonexistent.

Literacy is achieved when one is able to decipher, judge, and use many different kinds of text. One may be as easily enslaved to the high-minded texts of poets and philosophers as to more vulgar and demotic productions. Producers of texts correctly assume that their audiences will possess reading competence. But many text producers neither want nor expect anything more than a purely responsive act of reading—an act which will decode the transmission in precisely the way that the sender desires.

If messages and senders were innocent and reliable agents, this ideal of communication would be all that we would require. It is the ideal of advertisers, of course, as well as the ideal of all those who desire to create homogeneous and self-gratified audiences. The many texts produced by our government during the last nine years offer a rich archive of materials designed to short-circuit reflective and critical thought. For this very reason they are texts which reading teachers ought to use as often as possible: for they are texts which beautifully illustrate how communicators can manipulate their messages to create certain meanings and prevent others.

They are, in other words, texts which show us how and why we must read beyond the linear immediacies of their powerful propaganda.

I close with one final reflection on my original text, "Reagan's Farewell," which I have been treating as if it were authored by Reagan's media staff. In point of fact, "Reagan's Farewell" was put together, many different times, by the public media, by news institutions like ABC, CBS, NBC, and their local affiliates. If "Reagan's Farewell" is a ceremony of the news, the news machines more than cooperated in the presentation of that ceremony. "Reagan's Farewell" is, like any Shakespeare production (on stage *or* in a book), a social text. One of the more disturbing and grotesque "meanings" of "Reagan's Farewell" lies in its revelation of the fourth estate's susceptibility to propaganda manipulation. *This* particular meaning one would expect to be widely registered in our own society, where the idea of a free and critical press is founded at the deepest institutional levels. That it has not seemed an important meaning to many people, including people in the fourth estate, is yet another, and even darker, meaning to be found in the text of "Reagan's Farewell."

Even under the best of circumstances, messages and their senders are neither innocent nor completely reliable. This is why readers must be prepared to defend themselves against both the errors and the perversions of those who communicate with texts.

6

Pound's *Cantos*: A Poem Including Bibliography

IMAGINE for a moment that Pound's famous definition of epic—"a poem containing history"[1]—had been written before the eighteenth century and the subsequent development of modern critical historiography. (When earlier theories of epic call it the genre for celebrating heroic deeds, they are, in a sense, also seeing the epic as a poem containing history: for the common traditional view is that history is the record of the acts of great men.) A poem containing history, written in the twentieth century, means not simply "the tale of the tribe," but the self-conscious presentation of such a tale. It is therefore a poem which will have already theoretically imagined a critical edition of itself. A twentieth-century poem containing history will have to invent and display, somehow, at least the equivalent of footnotes, bibliography, and other scholarly paraphernalia.

This is, of course, to describe Pound's *Cantos* quite exactly, as well as a number of other famous modern epic ventures. The "history" in the *Cantos* is necessarily "critical history," not antiquarian or heroic history. As a consequence, the *Cantos* is a work which is constantly reflecting upon itself, and not simply in a meditative way.

The special character of the work's reflective structures appears if we propose a second imagination: a critical edition of

129

Pound's epic work. This is to imagine laying a second-order critical structure over a work that is itself *not* "precritical." It is to imagine a procedure that reflects upon the form of the original work (a poem containing history in the form of critical history). To imagine a critical edition, then, forces the realization that the bibliographical features of the *Cantos* are simultaneously features of the work's meaning. *How* the poem (or history) makes itself is a primary subject in the poem, as it is a primary subject for critical history.

Elsewhere I have discussed how the *Cantos* executes its historical, political, and ideological meanings.[2] This was an exercise in what philologists used to call higher criticism. Here I shall be pursuing a line of lower criticism. I want to explore *how* meanings operate at the work's most primary material levels. In carrying out this particular exercise, we shall trace an exemplary textual scene where the material forms and events of writing and printing call attention to the parts they play in the signifying system of the work.

I begin by looking at a few typical pages from the *Cantos* (see illus. 8). This represents a page from the first book installment of the *Cantos* project, *A Draft of XVI. Cantos* (1925). Although the illustration here is reproduced in black and white, the original was printed in red and black, with the decorated capital and the canto heading in red. This two-color printing style is maintained throughout the book. It was published by William Bird at the Three Mountains Press in Paris. Only a few of Pound's current readers are aware that Pound arranged and carefully oversaw the production of this book (and its uniform successor, *A Draft of the Cantos 17–27* [1928]). Most encounter the texts of the opening cantos in a much modified format. For example, see illustration 9. This is the first text page of Canto XIII as it appears in the standard New Directions text which we read today. This text follows the format of *A Draft of XXX Cantos* as it was published in 1933 by Farrar & Rinehart. The disappearance of the two-color printing and of the elaborate ornamental materials is only the most dramatic sign of a set of wholesale alterations in page layout, typeface, ink, and paper. We have moved from a decorated and hand-processed work toward one that bears all the insignia of what Walter Benjamin called "the age of mechanical reproduction."

The descent from the texts of 1925/1928—which culminate Pound's appropriation of his Pre-Raphaelite inheritance—to the industrial text of 1933 was not immediate. In 1930 Pound published his first complete edition of *A Draft of XXX Cantos* with the Hours Press in Paris. The opening page of Canto XIII in the 1930 edition appears as it does in illustration 10. In this 1930 text we are still in the world of fine printing, as the book's decorative capitals—all designed by Pound's wife, incidentally—show. These 1930 capitals possess a distinctive (clearly vorticist) style which mediates between the self-consciously antiqued physicalness of the 1925/1928 texts and capitals, and the more transparent trade edition texts of 1933 and thereafter.

The (uniform) title covering both the 1930 and the 1933 texts would eventually come to designate what we now rightly think of as the "first installment" of the *Cantos*. A single structure of thirty cantos replaced the earlier two-part structure which had come out as the "Draft of XVI. Cantos" and the "Draft of the Cantos 17–27." The incorporation of these first two parts into a single (and slightly larger) unit was perhaps foreshadowed by the unusual bibliographical coding shared by those two early decorated books. This matter is important, of course, because the *Cantos* (somewhat like *Don Juan*, but not at all like *The Prelude*) is a work comprised of—organized as—a series of distinct sequences whose distinctness was initially defined by the event of publication. An edition of the *Cantos* will want to preserve the integrity of those separate parts—which are, after all, devices for organizing the reading experience. New Directions and Faber and

THE
THIRTEENTH
CANTO

KUNG walked
by the dynastic temple
and into the cedar grove,
and then out by the lower river,
And with him Khieu Tchi
and Tian the low speaking
And "we are unknown," said Kung,
" You will take up charioteering?
Then you will become known,
" Or perhaps I should take up charioteering, or archery?
" Or the practice of public speaking?"

And Tseu-lou said, "I would put the defences in order,"

And Khieu said, "If I were lord of a province
I would put it in better order than this is."
And Tchi said, "I would prefer a small mountain temple,
" With order in the observances,
with a suitable performance of the ritual,"
And Tian said, with his hand on the strings of his lute
The low sounds continuing
after his hand left the strings,
And the sound went up like smoke, under the leaves,
And he looked after the sound:
" The old swimming hole,
" And the boys flopping off the planks,
" Or sitting in the underbrush playing mandolins."
And Kung smiled upon all of them equally.
And Thseng-sie desired to know:
" Which had answered correctly?"
And Kung said, " They have all answered correctly,
" That is to say, each in his nature."

8. Ezra Pound, *A Draft of XVI. Cantos* (1925), first page of
Canto XIII (originally printed in red and black, here reproduced
in monochrome).

俟夫子

KUNG walked
            by the dynastic temple
and into the cedar grove,
            and then out by the lower river,
And with him Khieu Tchi
            and Tian the low speaking
And " we are unknown, " said Kung,
" You will take up charioteering?
            Then you will become known,
" Or perhaps I should take up charioteering, or archery?
" Or the practice of public speaking? "
And Tseu-lou said, " I would put the defences in order, "
And Khieu said, " If I were lord of a province
I would put it in better order than this is. "
And Tchi said, " I would prefer a small mountain temple,
" With order in the observances,
            with a suitable performance of the ritual, "
And Tian said, with his hand on the strings of his lute
The low sounds continuing
            after his hand left the strings,
And the sound went up like smoke, under the leaves,
And he looked after the sound :
            " The old swimming hole,
" And the boys flopping off the planks,
" Or sitting in the underbrush playing mandolins. "
            And Kung smiled upon all of them equally.
And Thseng-sie desired to know :
            " Which had answered correctly? "
And Kung said, " They have all answered correctly,
" That is to say, each in his nature. "
And Kung raised his cane against Yuan Jang,
            Yuan Jang being his elder,
For Yuan Jang sat by the roadside pretending to
            be receiving wisdom.

. 57

9. Ezra Pound, *A Draft of XXX Cantos* (1930),
            first page of Canto XIII.

K XIII

Kung walked
        by the dynastic temple
and into the cedar grove,
        and then out by the lower river,
And with him Khieu Tchi
        and Tian the low speaking
And 'we are unknown,' said Kung,
'You will take up charioteering?
        'Then you will become known,
'Or perhaps I should take up charioteering, or archery?
'Or the practice of public speaking?'
And Tseu-lou said, 'I would put the defences in order,'
And Khieu said, 'If I were lord of a province
I would put it in better order than this is.'
And Tchi said, 'I should prefer a small mountain temple,
'With order in the observances,
        with a suitable performance of the ritual,'
And Tian said, with his hand on the strings of his lute
The low sounds continuing
        after his hand left the strings,
And the sound went up like smoke, under the leaves,
And he looked after the sound:
        'The old swimming hole,
'And the boys flopping off the planks,
'Or sitting in the underbrush playing mandolins.'
        And Kung smiled upon all of them equally.
And Thseng-sie desired to know:
        'Which had answered correctly?'
And Kung said, 'They have all answered correctly,
'That is to say, each in his nature.'
And Kung raised his cane against Yuan Jang,

62

10. Ezra Pound, *Cantos*: New Directions edition, tenth printing,
first page of Canto XIII.

Faber have always preserved the distinctions by printing the first thirty cantos as a single unit.[3]

But what about the decorated layout of the 1925/1928 text, or for that matter the fine printing of the 1930 Hours Press text? It is true that, by the time the work descended to the trade edition of 1933, the "first installment" of *Cantos* had abandoned what an anthropologist might call its "thick" original textuality. Should an edition of the *Cantos* restore the decorative texts of 1925, 1928, and 1930 to that unit of the *Cantos* we now call "A Draft of XXX Cantos"?

American textual scholarship has operated for about forty years under the following commandment: Thou shalt not mix literary criticism and editorial practice. In one of the recent issues of *Text*—the annual publication of the Society for Textual Scholarship—the commandment is issued yet again by several parties, including Bowers in his 1985 presidential address to the Society. In this case, however, the pronouncement is made in a context—the context of the particular issue of *Text*—where the authority of the reissued commandment is being, at the same time, questioned, attacked, or simply ignored.[4]

I bring up this matter of textual and editorial theory because the case of the *Cantos* illustrates in the most dramatic ways the difficulty, if not the impossibility, of separating textual/editorial work from critical/interpretive work. A decision about how to treat the physical presentation of Cantos 1–30 in an edition will drastically affect how the work is read and understood.

Furthermore, when we attempt to arrive at such a decision we will not be able to avoid literary-critical and interpretive analysis and argumentation. No matter how technical the discourse of bibliography and textual criticism becomes, it is ultimately a humane and not a technological pursuit, as A. E. Housman once so eloquently argued.[5] What Housman left unsaid, however, and what needs to be clearly understood today, is that the symbiosis of editorial and interpretive work only functions properly when the more materially oriented textual and bibliographical studies return the favor of interpretation's gifts to editors and editing.

We can see what is involved here if we consider for a moment the titles of the first three book installments of the *Cantos*: that is to say, the titles of the 1925, 1928, and 1930 texts. I am particularly interested in Pound's representation of the *number* of the cantos being issued. These are, in one simple sense, sixteen, eleven, and thirty cantos, respectively. But notice the way Pound's text represents these numerical facts. I leave aside altogether the frequently remarked word "Draft," which is extremely important of course, to call attention to the "XXX" of the 1930 text. Whether or not Pound added three cantos to the 1925/1928 unit in order to secure an arbitrary wordplay on the year of publication—something no one has suggested, so far as I am aware, even though such a textual/historical rhyme works very nicely in the event—the typographical form of the number is remarkable (even if it, too, has thus far gone *un*remarked).

The title of *A Draft of XXX Cantos* presents the concept of "thirty" neither in an English script nor even in arabic numerals, but in roman signs: XXX. This small detail is a visual cue calling attention to the linguistic importance of the material form of every script. That Pound was aware of the significance of the material form which signs assume (or are given) hardly needs emphasizing. Indeed, the different forms which Pound gives to numerical units in the titles of the 1925 and 1928 texts—roman and arabic, respectively—partly attract our notice by the differential they make with each other.[6]

The forms "thirty," "30," and "XXX," while equivalent at one level, at various other levels diverge into very different horizons of meaning. These differences would have remained invisible, however, had Pound chosen to represent the numerical value of these early books of cantos in the form of the common English script. Having been represented in print as "XXX" and not "thirty" (or even "30"), the work draws the reader's eye to the physique of the texts. Pound's use of roman and arabic numerals in these titles has the paradoxical effect of heightening our awareness of the peculiarity of the word "thirty," and makes of that word—which does not even put in an appearance here—an index of the sleep into which, in Pound's view, our common English scripts—which is to say the users of those scripts—have fallen. "XXX" is Pound's equivalent of Thoreau's call to wake his neighbors up: in this case, to wake them up to the reality and truth of language.

One of Pound's greatest contributions to poetry lies concealed in his attentiveness to the smallest details of his texts' bibliographical codes. Along with Mallarmé, Apollinaire, and many other modernist innovators, Pound felt that the renewal of the resources of poetry in an age of advanced mechanical reproduction required the artist to bring all aspects of textual production under the aegis of imagination.[7] Nothing was to be taken for granted: the poetry would be brought forth not simply at the linguistic level, but in every feature of the media available to the scriptural imagination.

More than any other of the early modernists, however, Pound was also keenly aware of the large sociohistorical horizon within which the codes of textual production necessarily existed. The scale of his textual vision appears with great clarity in the ornamental features of those early books of 1925, 1928, and 1930. We begin to see this by looking at the decorative initials which Dorothy Pound executed for the 1930 Hours Press edition. These initials, distinctly vorticist in style, comprise a bibliographical allusion to Pound's own earlier efforts to "gather the limbs of Osiris."[8] Pound's vorticism was one of the early forms that his modernist program took;[9]

before 1912 his work was still closely tied to the protomodernist innovations of those important late nineteenth-century movements, Pre-Raphaelitism and aestheticism.

The decorative materials in the 1925/1928 books also comprise an elaborate act of cultural allusion. In this case Pound's text is (as it were) thinking back through a signal event in book production, the founding of the Kelmscott Press by William Morris in March of 1891. In May, Morris issued his own prose romance *The Story of the Glittering Plain*, which was followed in October by his *Poems by the Way*. Like Pound's 1925/1928 texts, these books are distinguished by elaborate ornamental materials, including decorative capitals and two-color printing in red and black.[10]

To understand the full context of what was involved in Pound's act of bibliographical homage and allusion, we should recall the immediate historical background of the founding of Morris's Kelmscott Press.[11] The invention of chromolithography in 1816 was of course decisive, but its impact on decorative book production took some time to develop. The key textual events took place between 1849, when Henry Noel Humphreys completed *The Illuminated Books of the Middle Ages*, and 1861, when Emily Faithfull's Victoria Press brought out its first work, the decorated collection of stories titled *Victoria Regia*, with an introduction by Adelaide Ann Proctor. Proctor founded the Society for the Promotion of Employment for Women in 1860 as a result of hearing Ruskin lecture and of reading his work, and the Victoria Press—with its company of women compositors—was established under the aegis of the society.[12]

During the 1850s some of the key events were the appearance of Ruskin's *Stones of Venice* and the publication of several manuals teaching decorative book design and manuscript illumination. The Victoria Press emerged at a moment when the interest in decorative printing had become quite strong. Most of the work dealt directly with medieval and religious materials, but secular avenues also began to open up, as the printing of *Victoria Regia* itself shows. In 1857 Humphreys published his decorated *Sentiments and Similes of William Shakespeare* and Edward Moxon produced his *Illustrated Edition* of the selected poems of Tennyson. This last project drew upon the work of some of the leading young artists of the period, including D. G. Rossetti.

The interest in decorative book production thus fed directly into the work of the two key figures of the Pre-Raphaelite movement, Morris and D. G. Rossetti. In 1862 Rossetti designed the gold-stamped covers and supplied the material for his sister's decorated title page to *Goblin Market and other Poems*, and in 1870 Rossetti's own collection of poetry was produced with handsome endpapers designed by himself and beautifully ornamented covers. Morris's *Love is Enough* followed in 1872 in an edition produced with similar decorative features, and he made plans to reissue it with printing ornaments of his own design. These plans, however, had to be abandoned for lack of appropriate typefaces.

All of this activity forms the context in which the idea of the Kelmscott Press was eventually born. Behind it lay a consciousness that the passing of the fifteenth century marked an epochal European event. Pre-Raphaelite does not merely involve a gesture back to certain medieval styles of art, but to a period when craft-based production was a general feature of European life. The books coming out of the Kelmscott Press were meant to recall that historical moment when a newly discovered tool of mechanical reproduction—the printing press—had not yet become an engine of cultural alienation.

As we know, Kelmscott Press would have an immediate and immense influence on book production in England. During the thirty years after its founding, a whole series of presses, which specialized in fine and decorative printing, sprang up. However, like the Chiswick Press earlier, which produced manuals of illumination, books of heraldry, and so forth, these presses did not customarily print works of contemporary literature.[13] To the extent that they dealt in books with a relatively broad cultural interest, they issued decorative reprintings of older and often well-known works—classical texts that would recall Aldus Manutius and the other heroes of the printing revolution, or crucial medieval authors like Dante and Villon.

So far as Pound's work is concerned, then, the Victorian decorated book was most important for its medieval preoccupations. Many Victorian decorated books were produced which did not take their inspiration from an imaginative turn back to the Middle Ages, but it is the tradition which did make that turn that made its impact upon Pound. And the key figure in that tradition was, of course, William Morris.[14]

The Kelmscott Press Chaucer is a good example of this effort to make historicized aesthetic arguments via elaborate bibliographical means. But unlike the Chiswick Press earlier or most of the later printing houses that sprang up under its inspiration, Kelmscott Press began by publishing contemporary work, and it never abandoned that imagination of its mission. This is also important to remember, in relation to Pound's 1925/1928 *Cantos* books, because the historicist argument embedded in the Kelmscott *Story of the Glittering Plain* and the 1925/1928 edition of early cantos is emphasized by the contemporaneity of the work being printed.

The physique of Pound's 1925/1928 edition is thus not simply an allusion to Morris, Pre-Raphaelitism, and the recent history of decorative printing.[15] It is equally an allusion, *through them*, to the renaissance revolution in printing initiated in the fifteenth and sixteenth centuries. In this respect Pound's elaborate bibliographical coding rhymes with topics he raises and pursues at the work's linguistic levels—most dramatically, I suppose, in the famous allusion to the sixteenth-century printing house of Christian Wechel at the end of the first canto.

Pound's use of the physique of the book in his 1925/1928 edition of the early cantos consequently goes far beyond the bibliographical experiments of Mallarmé, Apollinaire, the vorticists, the imagists, and the futurists. In all the latter cases no programmatic effort is made to set these experiments in a world-historical scale. But this is exactly what Pound is trying to do, and his effort turns the *Cantos*, properly understood, into an epic project—and an epic project grounded in that horizon of cultural self-understanding which has dominated the twentieth century: Language. Pound's *Cantos* is an epic of language, with language conceived as a widely dispersed and world-historical set of different social, institutional, and material events.

II

The ambition of a project like the *Cantos* forced Pound to pay the closest attention to the semiotic potential which lay in the physical aspects of book and text production. We observe this attentiveness throughout his career—although after World War II his involvement with the printing processes of his works was largely confined to the editions put out by the Milanese firm of Scheiwiller. His typescripts—the setting copy for all his work, early and late—carefully compose the spatial relations of their characters, and, as such, these typescripts represent "directions for printing," as it were. In random comparisons I have made for the later cantos, the printed texts faithfully reproduce the spatial relations of the words and lines which appear in the typescripts. Furthermore, we will observe in the next chapter, in the case of *Hugh Selwyn Mauberley*, Pound's inclination to exploit the semiotic potential latent in the smallest bibliographical details of his books.

Implicit in all this is the understanding that language has many translinguistic communicative resources. Like so many of his contemporaries, Pound *as a writer* repeatedly imagines the page and the book the way a painter or a book designer would imagine it. This bibliographical imagination can be traced back through Pound's vorticism, to the Pre-Raphaelites, and—their point of modern departure—to William Blake.

At its most extreme form, this habit of perception can turn a page of text into a "wall of words"—which is the way one good contemporary reader of Blake has described the effect of many of the pages of his illuminated epics:[16] for example, the page from *Jerusalem* (see illus. 11). This text is very difficult to read. In fact, much of its force derives from the play our eyes and mind are driven to engage with each other, the contest of their shifting claims to authority over our reading experience. This text is breaking down the ordinary distinction readers and scholars make between, on one hand, "the [verbal] text," and, on the other, "the [visual] ornamentation." Like Coleridge when he received in a dream the full text of "Kubla Khan," Blake seems the producer of poetical works "in which all the images rose up before him as *things*, with a parallel production of the correspondent expressions": words as images, words as things.

In this respect, it is difficult to avoid the similarity of Blake's work to the books Morris turned out from his Kelmscott Press. We can see the connection, for example, when that distinguished historian of the book, Douglas McMurtrie, alludes to certain criticisms that have been raised against Morris's work:

> The criticism levelled by competent critics against the Kelmscott books holds that the fundamental purpose of books is to be read and that the Morris books are neither legible in their type matter nor convenient for handling in their format. They contend that they are, first, exercises in decorative design and only secondarily, books intended for reading; that even if one endeavors to read them, the mind is distracted from the sense of the author by spots or masses of decoration so insistent in area and color as to completely overshadow the text.[17]

11. William Blake, *Jerusalem* plate 17 (from Trianon Press facsimile edition of the Cunliffe copy, reproduced in monochrome).

"Even the most enthusiastic admirers of William Morris must admit that there is much of truth in these criticisms," Mc-Murtrie adds—to which one would perhaps want to reply, "True, but hardly true enough." For such "criticisms" miss one of the chief points that Blake and Morris are making about the translinguistic features of language. Because language is always materialized and embodied in one way or another, these material phenomena (they have an acoustic dimension as well) assume independent signifying functions. Poets like Blake, Morris, and Pound are bent upon the exploitation of the entirety of language's signifying mechanisms.

Pound's *Cantos* never neglect or abandon this signifying dimension of language. Nevertheless, his texts—like those of the Cuala Press, which so influenced his mind on these matters—definitely attempt to preserve the clear readability of the text.[18] He does not treat his pages as paintings or full-scale visual designs, which both Blake and Morris most certainly do.[19] Furthermore, after 1930 Pound no longer exploited the phanopoeic textual resources passed on to him through Pre-Raphaelitism: with one significant exception, all the parts of the *Cantos* published after 1930 are commercially produced.[20] (That exception, which I shall return to in a moment, involves the notorious "forbidden cantos," which were printed in Italy but not placed in sequence as Cantos 72–73 until 1989.)

If, after 1930, Pound leaves behind that highly decorative approach to the *Cantos* so spectacularly displayed in the 1925/1928 books, he does not by any means abandon his commitments to bibliographical coding for his work. Pound's Pre-Raphaelite cantos—and I do think Cantos 1–27 ought to be called that—signal important historical meanings, both in the development of European poetry at large, and in the more immediate context of Pound's (and modernism's) evolution. Pound's Pre-Raphaelite cantos are the equivalent of what Yeats did a few years later when he placed his free verse text of Pater's Mona Lisa at the outset of his *Oxford Book of Modern Verse.*

In the recession of the conventions of decorative book production from the post-1930 *Cantos* we continue to see Pound exploiting the bibliographical resources of commercial press printing. These effects appear most spectacularly whenever Pound introduces Chinese characters into a textual field dominated by Western scripts (refer to illustrations 3–7 in chapter 5). If such pages have been imagined as texts to be read, they are also being treated as visual constructions of printed characters. Looking and reading converge as reciprocal functions.

The effect, moreover, controls the signifying process at the macro as well as the micro level. Perhaps one's first impression, in seeing pages like this, is to register the gestalt of the figuration—the page treated as a "composition," with that term to be taken simultaneously as a typographer and as a painter would use it. But such effects of general page design are controlled by the way the text forces a reader to pay attention to the smallest detail.

In pages like these, for instance, the Chinese characters appear before our eyes with all the ideographic force that Pound, following Ernest Fenellosa, had discovered in them. They work this way because the characters are so unfamiliar to us. We have to remember, in reflecting on texts like this, that Pound's poem is written for a Euro-American audience, and that its rhetoric depends upon certain assumptions Pound makes about the language(s) that have descended to (and *into*) that audience in its historical emergence. If Pound's Chinese characters invoke the entire apparatus of Pound's Fenellosan approach to such materials, that conceptual framework only serves to focus our attention on the immediate text's smallest particularities. English and other Euro-American languages are the large field into which Pound has introduced his Chinese characters, but it is the latter which throw the details of that larger field into an entirely new perspective. To put it as simply as possible: the Chinese characters are an index of the kind of attention all scripted forms demand, even—and perhaps most crucially—those forms which are most familiar to us, such as the forms of our own languages. The Ming ideogram on page 539 (illustration 7), for example, is explicitly presented as the sign of an essential feature of signs in general: that they preserve "distinctions in clarity," and that every sign, even the smallest character of a language, must be attended to for the "distinctions" it draws.

The small superscripts which are attached to the English transliterations of the Chinese ideograms—for instance, the superscript "2" attached to "Ming" on page 539—are a good index of the presence of such distinctions at the phonic level of the Chinese language. Western translators of Chinese evolved a convention of four superscripts, numbered 1, 2, 3, 4, to designate different possible phonic values which a particular word might have. These four numbers represent Western translators drawing necessary distinctions of tonal value for different words; for in Chinese, the same written character is not absolutely self-identical, since it may stand for very different words (or perhaps we should say here "things") depending upon the tone in which it is uttered.[21]

But the words and characters of every language are never self-identical or transparent. One of the great objects of the *Cantos* is to reeducate Western readers in the use of their own inherited languages, in the understanding of how language works in general, and how materially and historically grounded are its meanings. Pound's use of Chinese characters dramatizes the presence of sharp distinctions in fields that might otherwise appear smooth and uniform. There are *differences* that have to be attended to, at the top of page 780 of the *Cantos*, in the way Pound repeats the Greek word *kalliastragalos*. There is uppercase and there is lowercase; there is English script and Greek script; there is even the placement of the repeated word at the center of the page, as well as the (perhaps fortuitous, but nevertheless equally significant) appearance of the repeated word at the top of the page in the received New Directions text.[22]

In this entire context, the problem of editing the *Cantos* becomes at one and the same time a problem of interpreting the work. This happens because the poem will not allow an editor to proceed on the assumption that final distinctions can be drawn, for example, between substantives and accidentals, between "the text" and its ornaments—between the work of the poet, on one hand, and the work of the compositor, the printer, even the bibliographer on the other. There is not first a text and then the meaning of a text. The transmission history of poetical work is as much a part of the poetry as is the "original" work of the author.

The relevance of the transmissive medium is particularly apparent when we consider the "forbidden cantos," the two sections (Cantos LXXII–LXXIII) which belong immediately before the Pisan Cantos. These two parts were kept out of the New Directions and Faber collected cantos until the tenth printing in 1986. At that point they are placed in the text out of sequence—near the end of the book, as a kind of appendix to the *Drafts and Fragments* section. Finally, in the eleventh printing (1989), the two cantos are printed in sequence after Canto LXXI.

The textual history of these two cantos is eloquent, a material sign in itself of why these texts have been called "the forbidden cantos." They were written in 1944 and first published in 1945 in two succeeding issues of the *Marina Repubblicana* (15 January and 1 February), a propaganda organ of Mussolini's Salo regime. They comprise an extended act of homage to Italy's (disintegrating) fascist government. The physical text of this first printing demonstrates with great force the way a verbal text and its printing medium can be made to interact and comment on each other.

When the new installment of Pound's *Cantos* was printed,

however, Cantos 72–73 were absent: the new group included only Cantos 74–84, and they appeared in print under the title *The Pisan Cantos*. The two fascist cantos were "forbidden" an entrance into the ongoing text, their subject matter being, in the immediate post-war context, both forbidding and forbidden. It is not clear to me whether Pound himself withheld Cantos 72–73 in 1948, or whether he was persuaded to do so by others. In any event, a new edition (with an augmented Canto 72) was printed for copyright purposes in 1973— probably just twenty-five were printed, and perhaps as few as three copies. Then, in 1983, the two cantos were printed complete by Vanni Scheiwiller with an introduction by Mary de Rachewiltz.

I narrate this printing history because each part of the history contains a proleptic explanation of the later parts. The 1986 New Directions text differs only in the most trivial ways from the 1983 text *so far as the linguistic level of the text is concerned*; and, whereas the texts of Canto 72 printed after 1945 are longer than that of the initial printing, the linguistic material, once it appears in print, preserves a noticeable stability. Nevertheless, the physical presentation of these two cantos is patently relevant to their "meaning." Cantos 72–73 are "forbidden cantos," for example, not by "author's intentions" but by historical and social circumstances, and those circumstances are preserved in the bibliographical codes through which the "forbidden cantos" have been transmitted to us.

The most recent phase of this textual history was inaugurated in 1989 when New Directions issued its eleventh printing of the *Cantos*. In this new format Cantos 72–73 are moved once again, this time to a position just before the Pisan Cantos, where their numeration would indicate they ought to be placed. Perhaps they have at last come to rest. In any case, their wanderings comprise an important feature of their meaning and their textual history, and any scholarly edition of the entire work will have to highlight such matters.

III

Pound's *Cantos* dramatize, on an epic scale, a related pair of important truths about poetry and all written texts: that the meaning of works committed into language is carried at the bibliographical as well as the linguistic level, and that the transmission of such works is as much a part of their meaning as anything else we can distinguish about them. Transmission is an elementary kind of translation, a reenactment (and often one kind of completion) of the poetical act which the artist sets in motion. That Pound understood these matters is clear from his deep involvement with the material transmissions of his work, as we have seen.

I should not conclude this discussion, however, without recalling Dante Gabriel Rossetti; for Rossetti, like Morris, was one of the first to speak in this particular modernist tongue, though he did so—also like Morris—in a distinctly Victorian dialect. Not only is Rossetti's book of translations, *The Early Italian Poets* (1861), one of modernism's seminal (if forgotten) points of reference and departure, his various "Sonnets for Pictures" forecasts the modernist attempt to break away from one hundred years of symbolist thinking about art and language, with its implicit (or even explicit) ideological distinction between poetry and the meaning of poetry. The "Sonnets for Pictures" represents Rossetti's understanding that the work of art (poem or painting) and its meaning are not two but one thing. Meaning in art does not require an attendant hermeneutical operation to be revealed. Far from being an absent or precious secret, art's meaning is present and manifest. It is the act and eventuality of the work itself.

The function of criticism, in such circumstances, is an enabling one—to facilitate as immediate and direct an experience of the work as possible. Blake called it cleansing the doors of perception. In Rossetti it appears as an explicit critique of the hermeneutical and symbolist program. His "Sonnets for Pictures" aspires to the condition of pictorial concreteness: words as characterological figures, words as images in need of no further interpretation. It is phanopoeia and ideography in a Victorian mode:

> This is that blessed Mary, pre-elect
>   God's Virgin.
>
> ("Mary's Girlhood")
>
> Here meet together the prefiguring day
> And day prefigured.
>
> ("The Passover in the Holy Family")[23]

The method is clear from the way Rossetti uses terms like "pre-elect" and "prefiguring." These are interpretation's words, but Rossetti's poetry offers them to us as if they stood on the same plane of meaning as the visual figures he also presents:

> John binds the shoes
> He deemed himself not worthy to unloose;
> And Mary culls the bitter herbs ordained.
>
> ("The Passover in the Holy Family")

In such texts meaning becomes another concrete detail, for the poetry is working to transform symbols back into an original concreteness. Rossetti's sonnet "Mary's Girlhood" does not represent itself as an "interpretation" of the original picture, but as the picture's verbal equivalent: *ut pictura poiesis*, a making like a picture. It strives to eliminate the gap that the symbolic imagination had opened between the *figura* and its interpretation.

Rossetti's purpose emerges with unmistakable clarity in his second (untitled) sonnet on his picture *Mary's Girlhood*. This sonnet devotes itself entirely to an exegesis of the painting's symbolical *figurae*:

> These are the symbols. On that cloth of red
>   I' the centre is the Tripoint: perfect each,
>   Except the second of its points, to teach

> That Christ is not yet born. The books—whose head
> Is golden Charity, as Paul hath said—
>> Those virtues are wherein the soul is rich:
>> Therefore on them the lily standeth, which
> Is Innocence, being interpreted.

Here symbolism is being naively recovered at the level of pure perception. Meaning thus rises up before us as a set of apparitional details, as it does in Rossetti's sonnet "For An Allegorical Dance of Women by Andrea Mantegna." In the latter, however, Rossetti explicitly comments on the kind of art he is trying to imagine, the kind of meaning he is trying to expose, when he concludes his sonnet in this way:

> It is bitter glad
> Even unto tears. Its meaning filleth it,
> A secret of the wells of Life: to wit:—
> The heart's each pulse shall keep the sense it had
> With all, though the mind's labour run to nought.

The "secret" meaning of this art is its perduring sensoriness, which does not have to be sought beneath the appearances of things, through the abstracted "labour" of the mind.

Essential to the force of the passage is the "wit" playing about Rossetti's line, "A secret of the wells of Life." The phrase recalls the symbolistic commonplace, that truth is only found at the bottom of a well. Rossetti's text, however, teases from the word "wells" an unexpected metonymic significance; for the text has exposed another possible meaning of the word "wells," a meaning more connected to the words "tears" and "filleth" which immediately precede the phrase. The great "secret of the wells of Life" may not lie concealed at the bottom, it may rather "well" at the top, like a brimming cup, or like eyes filled with tears. One recalls Blake's proverb of Hell—"The cistern contains, the fountain overflows"—because Rossetti, like Blake from whom he learned so much, wanted to recover an art of ornamental profusion, an art whose meaning is no more (and no less) than the actual and determinate play of the energetic mind.

This is exactly the inheritance received and passed on by Ezra Pound, and by those other modernists who followed similar constructivist lines: not so much Frost and Stevens and Eliot, as Stein and Williams and Zukofsky.

Beyond the Valley of Production; or,

De factorum natura: A Dialogue

[Interlocutors: J. J. Rome, Anne Mack, Georg Mannejc]

> Not that I agree with everything that I said in this essay. There is
> much with which I entirely disagree. The essay simply represents an
> artistic standpoint, and in aesthetic criticism attitude is everything.
> . . . A Truth in Art is that whose contradictory is also true.
> —OSCAR WILDE, "The Truth of Masks"

> But then the fact's a fact—and 'tis the part
> Of a true poet to escape from fiction.
> —BYRON , *Don Juan* Canto VIII

JJR: It was a fine lecture—at once learned, elegant, and imaginative. He even sketched the late nineteenth-century revolution in
decorated book production, and described the links—really,
the unbroken continuity—between that history and the visual
aspects of key works produced in the early modernist period
between 1910 and 1930. He wanted to show that the first two
book installments of Pound's *Cantos*—Cantos 1–16 were
published in 1925 and Cantos 17–27 in 1928—were at once
an apotheosis and final transcendence of the work done by
William Morris and the Kelmscott Press, Charles Ricketts and
the Vale Press, Lucien Pissarro and the Eragny Press—Doves
Press, Cuala Press, Unicorn Press, Ovid Press, publishers like

John Lane, Day and Son, William Mosher, and so many others that trace themselves, in the nineteenth century, back to Blake and the Chiswick Press. The intimate relation between book production and textual meaning—that is, the hermeneutic significance of book production economics, on one hand, and all the material aspects of "the text" on the other: these matters were brought forward until one could not evade the general conclusion he was trying to argue that between the emergence of the Pre-Raphaelite movement and 1930, the literary text was consistently being imagined and executed as a *social* text in the most material way.[1]

And of course an even larger argument was always suggesting itself. The farthest thing from McGann's mind was the idea that this history of decorated texts was a special case. The lecture assumed the audience's knowledge of his sociohistorical interpretive approach to nondecorated textual production throughout the nineteenth century, as well as his more general work on "theory of texts"—for instance, the detailed arguments for a theory of texts as comprising a double helix of grammatological and bibliographical codes, or the more recent elaboration of the three forms of "reading" (linear, spatial, and radial). And all this in the still larger context of the parallel work being carried out by others—Robert Darnton, Donald McKenzie, and the large group of people now working in the fields of cultural studies and literary pragmatics, or the smaller group of scholars (people like Michael Warren, Randall McLeod, Stephen Urkowitz) who have been exploding our imagination of the Shakespearean texts.

AM: What an enthusiast you are! McKenzie's work, to me, is "confused in argument," and I have no patience at all with his "politicizing of scholarship." As for McGann, I remain unpersuaded by his polemical schemes. "Up to now his effectiveness has been seriously undercut by a lack of rigorous thought, at least as reflected in his often careless prose."[2] The best part of the lecture was the part you left out entirely—that brief inter-

154

lude when he engaged the specific example of *Hugh Selwyn Mauberley*.

Pound was of course well aware of the semiotic potential which lay in the physical aspects of book and text production. One of his most famous poems—the imagist manifesto "In a Station of the Metro"—has been reprinted and commented upon many times, but because scholars have not gone back to the original printing of the poem, none have recognized the extreme performativity of this text as originally conceived.

The poem was first printed in Harriet Monroe's new magazine *Poetry* along with eleven other short poems by Pound. Of these eleven poems, ten appear in standard typographical form—but not "In a Station of the Metro." This, the last of the series printed, appears in the following unusual typographical format:[3]

IN A STATION OF THE METRO
The apparition   of these faces   in the crowd   :
Petals   on a wet, black   bough   .

The arrangement of the text's signs distinctly recalls Pound's typewriting habits—especially in the extended spacing before the final punctuation marks. Pound regularly left this kind of spacing before various marks of punctuation in his typescripts. The point to be emphasized, however, is that he did not *regularly* carry this habit over to the printed texts.

Pound himself (not Harriet Monroe) was almost certainly responsible for the performative typography of "In a Station of the Metro." In any case, we know he took an active part in the physical presentation of many of his later texts. The case of *Hugh Selwyn Mauberley* is especially interesting. This book was published by John Rodker's Ovid Press in 1920. Rodker was an important figure on the scene of modernism as both a writer and a producer of some key modernist books, including Eliot's *Ara Vos Prec* (also published in 1920) as well as the first two book installments of Pound's *Cantos*.

An extant set of corrected proof sheets of *Hugh Selwyn Mauberley* displays Pound's recurrent directions to the printer about minor details of the text's physical presentation. Next to the half title Pound writes "? higher in page," and the motto page has two of his notes: "T[op] of margin shd always be narrower than bottom. even excessively so." and next to the motto: "Set higher in page." On page 10 (the opening page of section "II. The Age Demanded") Pound circles the printer's handwritten number 10 at the top and pulls it to the bottom with the note: "numerals at bottom of page." Once again Pound adds a note for the placement of the page's block of type: "Set Higher."[4]

Perhaps the most startling typographical intervention was made in Pound's manipulation of the book's decorated capitals. *Hugh Selwyn Mauberley* was designed to have these ornamental initials (made by the artist Edward Wadsworth) at the beginning of each new section of the work. In the published book, however, there is one deviation from the pattern: the initial letter on page 16 (the "Brennbaum" section) is an italic capital, not a decorated capital. The letter is the letter "T" (the "Brennbaum" section opens with the line, "The skylike limpid eyes").

Let me begin by stating in simple declarative terms the significance of that italic capital, so far as Pound was concerned. It constituted a bibliographical allusion to what Pound called the practices of "old printers" who, when they ran out of decorated initials, would use "plain capitals or italics" instead. The italic capital was a deliberate moment of modernist constructivism in the text—a moment which, by breaking from the pattern of the decorated capitals, called attention to the book's self-conscious imitation of decorated book production. A good part of the satire in the poem operates through

the bibliographical code consciously deployed at the typographical level of the work. The physique of *Hugh Selwyn
Mauberley* raises an image of an artistic practice that would
triumph over all that "The Age Demanded." The fact that
this work, this book, is itself a part of what "the age demanded" only underscores the extremity of Pound's satiric
idealism.

How shall I persuade you that this "reading" of the italic
capital on page 16 is not simply my personal interpretive fan-
tasia? The answer is, by laying out the scholarly evidence.
The extant proofs of the book are now in the Rodker collection of the Humanities Research Center (HRC) at the University of Texas. They are a composite set, with two pages from
an earlier proof (i.e., received pages 21 and 22 containing the
sections "Envoi [1919]" and "1920 [Mauberley]").

Collation of the HRC composite proof with the first edition shows that at least one more proof of the text must have
been made. This fact is apparent not least of all from the decorated capitals in the proof. In a number of cases these do not
correspond to the letter called for by the text, and in each of
these instances Pound crosses out the wrong capital and indicates the proper letter (i.e., on pages 12 and 13, where the
printer had put decorated capitals "F" and "L", respectively).

In order to print *Hugh Selwyn Mauberley* according to the
design program evidently decided upon, the printer needed
five decorated Ts. He needed one for the first letter of each of
the following sections of the poem: sections III, IV, V,
"Brennbaum," and "1920 (Mauberley)," corresponding to
pages 11, 12, 13, 16, and 22, respectively. However, during
his initial course of typesetting the printer seems to have had
access only to two decorated Ts. He used one to set the type
on the separate earlier proof of pages 21 and 22, while on the
other set of coherent proofs—the main body of the extant
material, which includes pages 11, 12, 13, and 16—he only
puts a decorated T on page 11.

In correcting the proofs Pound noted the three instances where the printer put the wrong decorated capital (i.e., on pages 12, 13, and 16). So, for example, the decorated initial on page 12, which is wrongly an F, is corrected by Pound, and at this point he adds the significant note in the margin: "Use plain capitals or italics as in H. S. Mauberley [i.e., as in the italic half title]. The old printers did this when fancy capitals ran out."[5] Similarly, the decorated initials in the HRC proof for pages 13 and 16 are not Ts; Pound indicates the proper letter in each case, and on page 13 has this note: "Supply of Ts ran out."

But if Rodker's printer did not have his five decorated Ts when he was actually setting the type at the first two proof stages, he must have had access to the five at the final stage of printing. When the book appeared, four of the five Ts were decorated capitals, the fifth being the italic capital which is the central subject of this discussion. It is important that the italic capital in this case should appear on page 16, because in that position one becomes aware of the character's arbitrary placement. That is to say, in the final printed text the single, undecorated T does not come as the last in the sequence of initial Ts (the last is on page 22), but as the next to last, on page 16.

One might conclude, from this bibliographical anomaly, that Rodker's printer finally and in *fact* had only four decorated T initials, and that the undecorated T appears on page 16 because *in the final printing sequence* page 16 was the last to be corrected. Page 22, that is to say, already had its decorated T, as we can tell from the extant (early) proof of pages 21 and 22. This theory of the text might be supported from Pound's marginal note next to his page 13 correction of the decorated T: "Supply of Ts ran out."

When Pound wrote that note, however, the proofs he was correcting suggested that the "supply of Ts" had run out with the setting of page 11, not the setting of page 13. However, the note probably does not mean to indicate that Pound thought the "supply of Ts" had run out after page 13. Rather, it must be a general note, indicating his belief—after having had to correct two successive decorated capitals (on pages 12 and 13)—that Rodker's printer had only two decorated Ts.

But we know from the final printed text of *Hugh Selwyn Mauberley* that the printer had—in the end at any rate—access to at least four decorated Ts. Furthermore, we know from other evidence that the printer could have put decorated Ts for all five of the initials on pages 11, 12, 13, 16, and 22. We know this because the Ovid Press edition of Eliot's *Ara Vos Prec* prints each poem with the same set of decorated initials designed by Edward Wadsworth, and in this book six ornamental Ts are needed. All are present in the printed text.

This narrative has involved a thorny mass of detail, so let me summarize its significance from my immediate point of view. Evidently Pound assumed, when he was correcting the HRC proofs, that there were only two decorated Ts in the printer's shop, and on that assumption he imagined a way to make the deficiency a "meaningful" element in the text of the work. In the end, although *Hugh Selwyn Mauberley* could have been printed with five ornamental Ts, a decision was made to leave one of those Ts undecorated, thereby introducing into the typography a symbolic moment it would have otherwise lacked. Tiny as it is, that moment—by the differential it represents—does more to call attention to the work's general bibliographical codes than perhaps any other feature of the text.

More than that, however, the bibliographical moment only functions because of the general historical allusion it entails. *Hugh Selwyn Mauberley* is a satire on the tawdry world of cultured London immediately after the Great War. The 1920 Ovid Press edition, by the symbology of its carefully crafted printing, means to comment on the debasement of art and imagination in the contemporary and commercial world of England; and it means to develop its commentary by aligning itself with what it sees as other, less debased cultures. Pound's poetic sequence is well aware of the limits and ineffectualities of the Pre-Raphaelite inheritance—including the inheritance of the decorated book which the Pre-Raphaelites passed on. Nevertheless, his work is also aware of the faith which the Pre-Raphaelite tradition had kept with those earlier European cultural traditions that Pound saw as less debased and less commercially driven. The italic T on page 16 is not merely Pound's allusion to certain "old printers," it is the index of a massive act of reverential recollection which is being executed in *Hugh Selwyn Mauberley*.

AM: A nice piece of scholarly detective work, that.

JJR: And nicer still, to my mind, because its scholarship is carried out in a consciously invoked hermeneutical horizon. The archival materials and bibliographical analysis fund a larger interpretive and critical program.

AM: True enough—or maybe what you say is *too true*. I mean, McGann's contemporary polemic is so insistent, even messianic, as if he had a mission to rescue the study of poetry from the suffocated enclosures of his various theoretical antagonists: from the New Critics, the structuralists, the intertextualists, the deconstructivists. And, yet, what has this kind of "historical" criticism done except bring certain new kinds of materials—archival and historical materials—within that same suffocating hermeneutic circle? Memory itself is now being consumed by the aesthetic imagination.

JJR: In this respect, surely, the criticism replicates Pound's own work. Like the *Cantos, Hugh Selwyn Mauberley* is a "poem including history," a poem which gives an aesthetic habitation to both past and contemporary historical materials. The criticism operates in the same spirit that the author writ.

AM: Not exactly in the same spirit. It is true, of course, that

Pound and McGann both assume the textual foundation of historical understanding: that we can only "know" history through (and as) the texts which deliver it into our hands. It is also true that both are textual materialists, as it were—readers (and writers) whose "texts" are always social, institutional, and *materialized* in specific ways by particular people under specific conditions. But the similarities end there. Pound's work "remembers" certain facts about book production, for example, as part of a general memorializing act in which the present is analyzed and critiqued by the past. Like Blake's illuminated work of a hundred years before, *Hugh Selwyn Mauberley* is initially imagined and produced as an act of social resistance against an evolving age of mechanical reproduction and its one-dimensional men.

The resistance is raised at the textual level because, in Pound's mind, the immediate world is conditioned by how we receive the past: by *the way* the past is read, as well as *what* from the past is read. The Ovid Press edition of Pound's work—like the first twenty-seven cantos in their original boards—thickens and materializes the text's immediate moment of self-representation. In that very act the work sketches a critical history for the text as it appears before us. It exposes the historical deficiencies imaged (and imagined) in the mass-produced book. Pound's ornamented book is a commentary on the mass-produced book; and book production itself—whether mechanical or handcrafted—becomes, through the poem, the chief emblem and focus of a debased or a healthy social imagination.

JJR: But all that could just as well be said of McGann's criticism—indeed, it seems to me that McGann himself has said (more or less) exactly the same thing, somewhere or other.

AM: But the horizon within which McGann says these things is different. His work is scholarly and descriptive, not critical. What he does may be called literary criticism but it is really nothing more than literary interpretation: that is to say, it is the consumption and reproduction of our institutionalized literary codes (of their materials, means, and modes of production). As I said earlier, it simply offers a new way to pay old debts—a new way to expand the range of institutionalized hermeneutics. It is new historicism with a materialist face.

JJR: But what is it that you want from literary studies—that they become the locus of general social change, if not revolution? So far as the recent "turn to history" is concerned, surely it is enough, as Catherine Gallagher and others have said, that these new literary interests have made deep inroads into the schools and their curricula: "introducing non-canonical texts into the classroom . . . making students more aware of the history and significance of . . . imperialism, slavery, and gender differentiation in Western culture."[6] These are localized social changes, it is true, but because they are taking place within the state's chief ideological apparatus, their effects may be deep and far-reaching.

AM: It comes back to Marx's eleventh thesis on Feuerbach once again, does it not: "The philosophers have only *interpreted* the world in various ways; the point, however, is to *change* it." And at the moment I do not even ask for evidence of significant social change in society at large. Suppose we consider only the academy; or, even more particularly, those special academic regions where cultural literacy is defined and reproduced.

Literary interpretation is one dominant function of education in the human sciences, but the turn to sociohistorical studies has not really altered that function in any significant way. New historicism, materialist or otherwise, is a new set of interpretive procedures. They are being executed, however, entirely within the established social conventions and protocols of "literary studies." It is Stanley Fish's awareness of this situation—his clear view of the ways in which our established "interpretive communities" operate—which leads him to his avuncular remarks on what he has recently called "the young and the restless" left-liberal historical scholars. His soap opera epithet is an excellent index of his general argument: that literary studies today is a professional career whose truth-function is (and is to be) measured by personal success (or, in the jargon of the schools, the ability to persuade the interpretive community of one's peers that one is doing work that is professionally interesting and rewardable).[7]

To interpret the world in various ways, *within the horizon of a community of professional interpreters,* is to carry out the expected and well-established social functions of the group. It is to reinvest the credentials of the group. Furthermore, since this group functions to (re)produce the ideological needs of the state and society at large, its interpretations serve to *con*serve those larger social formations.

GM: But surely—may I enter this conversation for a moment?—everyone now is aware of those limitations. Or do you think that educators and professors are doomed to exhaust themselves and their interpretive acts in careerism or even professionalism? To imagine these things dominating personal or social action is to submit to what Roberto Unger calls "false necessity."[8] And if hermeneutic activity is socially conservative, do you believe that there are *no* aspects of "those larger social formations" which we might do well to conserve? Is the "larger social formation"—are our institutions of letters themselves—wholly and hopelessly debased, in every aspect, root and branch?

Besides, such an absolute distinction between "interpreting" and "changing" something reifies an illusion which a materialist theory of texts is specially armed to expose, as if "interpretation" did not involve specific acts carried out, under particular circumstances, and executed *as* certain determinate material forms. Roland Barthes, for some good reasons and to great effect, urged readers in 1971 to move "from work to text."[9] He did so because he wanted to alter our imagination of the literary "work" as a finished and self-defined "thing."

His move ushered in what some now think of as the final phase of that idealist program in hermeneutics stretching from Kant and Coleridge on one end, to Gadamer and Derrida on the other.

But for about ten years now we observe readers and writers turning against the Barthesian current and urging us to move "from text to work."[10] Implicit here is an argument to reimagine the term "work" in "textual" terms, and the term "text" in material terms. We do not have to follow Barthes in defining a literary "work" as a closed or finished system. The work named *Hugh Selwyn Mauberley*, for example, comprises a determinate and ongoing series of specific textual productions. Pound has a hand in some but by no means all of these productions. Besides, even for the texts of this poem that he was directly involved with—these include texts printed in 1920 (two texts here), 1921, 1926, 1949, and 1955—the poem's character, even its simple typographical character, changes and shifts.[11]

In the same way, we may think of a "text" as something else—something more determinate—than the fluid medium for free interpretive play which Barthes had imagined. The "text" one *works with* is particular and material, even in the case where one's attention is focussed on a certain set of texts: for example, the set of the texts of *Hugh Selwyn Mauberley* which Pound was directly, and more or less deeply, involved with.

But all this may and must be said of literary work in general, which necessarily appears as a series of particular texts produced and reproduced in different times and places for different uses and ends.

JJR: And the consequence of what you are saying, for interpretation, is twofold: first, present "meaning" is shown to emerge from an immediate dialogue with certain concrete social acts carried out in (and handed down from) the past; and second, those acts are multiple, so that determinate choices must be made about how and where to engage with this multiple past. As such, then, scholarship and literary studies would have to be judged neutral with respect to the issue of whether they are reactionary, conservative, liberal, or radical. The event is determined by particular choices that are made, roads taken and not taken.

AM: How agreeable and sanguine you both sound in your Heideggerian conversation. Yet it seems to me that you forget—I shall use one of your own favorite code words—the "particular" character of *literary* work (by which *I* mean—as I take it that you also mean—imaginative works and their secondary critical treatments).

No doubt [speaking to GM], Coleridge *was* the romantic ideologue you have suggested, but he understood, at any rate, that works of imagination deal with opposite and discordant qualities. The instance of *Hugh Selwyn Mauberley*, which you bring forward, will do as well as any. I mean, if that poem works to satirize contemporary culture by raising an alternative model of imaginative production, it equally dismantles its own ideological representations. That italic T in the "Brennbaum" section, which you and McGann find so elegant and intelligent, could as well be made the locus for an alternative, and antithetical, critical meditation.

I recall your attention to those multiple printings of the work you mentioned—one in 1920 preceding the Ovid Press edition, and at least four later printings. None of them display the decorative symbology of the Ovid Press edition. All are, in fact, dominated by the conventions of mechanical book production. Neither Pound nor his poem has any difficulty being translated into that (presumably) foreign and evil tongue. In the case of Pound's poem, this event seems all the more shocking because *Hugh Selwyn Mauberley*, as "initially" produced (forgive the irresistible pun), had—as you say—made such a symbolic parade of its typographic materials. In the end Pound's poem does not merely succumb to what "the age de-

165

manded," it emerges, like *The Waste Land*, as the very epitome of that age and the demands it made.

JJR: This argument is a far cry from your original presentation
of *Hugh Selwyn Mauberley* as a satire of cultural resistance.

AM: I do not recant that view; I am merely saying that other
views of the work become possible—become necessary—
when the scale of one's attention is changed. If we look at the
poem strictly in terms of the Ovid Press edition, we will be
inclined to see it in a certain way. But if we read it in the horizon of all its authoritative printings, the poem becomes a very
different work.

Much more could be said on these topics. For instance,
Pound's entire involvement with the decorated book was, as
you yourselves have noted, part of a large historical argument
he was making about the history of Western culture. He was,
in this respect, continuing the work of certain Victorians, but
especially Browning, Ruskin, and Morris. The first twenty-
seven cantos are simply *Hugh Selwyn Mauberley* in a fully
elaborated form—in the same way that *Prometheus Unbound*
is the "Ode to the West Wind" in its complete version, as it
were. Cantos 1–27 are also produced through John Rodker, in
two books even more lavishly printed and decorated than the
original *Hugh Selwyn Mauberley*. Furthermore, Cantos 1–27
make book production an explicit subject and theme at the
semantic level, and they connect it back to the early history of
book production in the West, and in Italy especially, between
the fourteenth and the sixteenth centuries.

That connection, however, only further destabilizes the
Cantos project. Like *Hugh Selwyn Mauberley*, the first
twenty-seven cantos moved east of their initial decorative and
ideographical Eden. This fall into the quotidian world took
place between 1925, when Three Mountains Press brought
out *A Draft of XVI. Cantos* in Paris, and 1933, when Farrar
& Rinehart published its trade edition of *A Draft of XXX
Cantos*. As with *Hugh Selwyn Mauberley*, these biblio-

graphical transformations trace the work's descent from craft to commerce. But in the case of the *Cantos*, the symbolic-cultural distinction between decorative and commercial book production is undermined by the historical lines which the *Cantos* draw between Renaissance bookmaking and Renaissance capitalism. The *Cantos'* historical materials do not permit the clear distinction, which the work itself offers, between late fourteenth-century Italian commerce and early twentieth-century European commerce. Indeed, the *Cantos'* own commitment to a historical imagination works to connect rather more than to disconnect the two.

Works of imagination like Pound's traffic in opposition because poetry—unlike any other form of discourse—is committed to the presentation of "opposite and discordant qualities." The integrity of that commitment can be measured by the way such works bring their own most cherished ideological visions into contradiction.

Furthermore—and this is for me the crucial point—by opening themselves to such radical self-alienation, imaginative work escapes the happy valley of production and consumption. The latter, which is technically called a restricted economy, is the dynamic underlying hermeneutics and the basis of the hermeneutical imagination of literature. In this context, one has to grant contemporary materialist historicisms like McGann's a certain usefulness. They help to expose the presence of this production/consumption dynamic operating at the superstructural level. Baudrillard, of course, has analyzed the same dynamic in his theoretical studies of "the mirror of production."[12]

Hermeneutics operates a restricted economy by producing "meaning" for general social consumption. It does this by conceiving the object of its studies, the poem, as a producer of meanings which can be consumed (because the meanings are determinate) and reproduced. The cycle is imagined to be endless and self-replicating. The ceaseless reproductions carried out under deconstructive signs, as Baudrillard has shown, merely reinstall the original productive model of the text.

I would oppose this hermeneutic imagination of imaginative work to a properly textual imagination. The latter corresponds to what has been called a "general economy," which is an economy of luxury and waste, of gift and loss. In this economy, acts of writing are not mirrored by (or in) acts of reading. "Meaning," the goal of interpretation, is alienated from writing in the realization that all texts are alienated from themselves. They are carnivals, masquerades, superfluities. From a purely productive vantage, they are useless. In that very uselessness, however, lies the ground of their (radical) critique of the quotidian orders of getting and spending.[13]

So far as Ezra Pound is concerned, we will come to see his poetry as itself part of the waste(d) world his work was conceived to oppose. Pound very definitely committed his writing to the service of restricted economies—to use functions and (American) pragmatistic ends. But in choosing poetry as his principal medium of exchange, he doomed his work to self-contradiction. His commitments to power, will, and control would reveal themselves as an astonishing luxury of waste, fragmentariness, and incoherence.

JJR: What is "useless" about that—or about carnivals and masquerades? Your distinction between restricted and general economies seems to me far to restrict*ive*. Ceremonies of luxury and waste are "useless" only in the narrow perspective of (say) Plato's *Republic* and *Laws*. Indeed, when utilitarian and pragmatic imaginations dominate, poetry's "use functions" emerge more clearly than ever—as Shelley, for one, has shown (in the *Defence of Poetry*).

And I also object to your sharp distinction between "poetry" and "interpretation": as if the two were not completely interinvolved. You yourself have been talking about the ideological purposes invested in *Hugh Selwyn Mauberley*. But the interpretive voice of literary criticism is an echo of the sense of

the poetry it reads. As such, interpretation—whether it is her-
meneutically charged (like De Man's studies), or empirically
oriented (like McGann's)—reimagines the works which come
into its hands.

Of course one could think of hermeneutics as the "science"
of poetry's "nature," the vehicle by which the hidden secrets
of an originary existence are translated into knowable and
usable forms. Nor would I even object to *this* model, misleading as it can be, so long as one does not employ it to equate the
terms "science" and "truth." One of the great (historical) vir-
tues of the hermeneutic appropriation of the "science model"
of experience and understanding lies exactly in the way it un-
dermines the positivist inertia of the scientific imagination of
the world. In this sense, hermeneutics can be imagined as the
science of the *un*knowing of scientistic illusions of truth. In
vulgar terms: because meaning and truth are imaginations of
those things, every science (including hermeneutics) is a way
of knowing that subsists on the edge of its own falsifiability.
The knowledge of both "nature" and "poetry"—that is to say,
the activities of "science" and "hermeneutics"—ought to replicate their originary heterocosms at the level of mind and self-
consciousness.

GM: I see you are not one who goes in fear of abstractions.
Come on—what we want to know is *how* precisely this dynamic of unknowing operates—and, even more to the point,
how it could possibly be called a form of knowledge.

Two broad lines of explanation have recommended themselves. The first, brilliantly pursued and elaborated during the
last twenty years of his life by Paul De Man, reads literature as
a mechanism of disillusionment. The self-alienation of imaginative texts becomes the means by which readers find their
interpretive moves weighed in the balance and found wanting.
This immediate and positive deconstruction of the reader,
consistently executed, reveals the ontological and "quasi-
objective" truth of personal knowledge and subjective experi-

ence. In Byron's summary and paradoxical words: "All that we know is, nothing can be known" (*Childe Harold's Pilgrimage* II. 56). Byron's statement is useful, in this context, just because of its deceptive poetic simplicity. Both grammar and rhetoric carry a clear performative illustration of how general and even assured knowledge can be made, literally, out of "nothing." De Man arrives at similar views by more abstract and circuitous methods. According to him, the failures and *aporias* of knowledge become the ground for a positive metaphysics by which the mind is able "to give rational integrity to a process [i.e, the blindness/insight dynamic] that exists independently of the self."[14]

According to this line of explanation, however, that self-independent "process" is the insight (and construct) of what Wordsworth once called "Reason in her most exalted mood" (*Prelude* XIV. 192). The process is revealed from the individual mind's specific acts of critical self-reflection—in De Man's terms, from its reflective engagements with particular literary texts. For this "science" of criticism, however, the question arises: What is the "nature" being pursued, what is the "object" of the knowing process? Or, to put the problem in Blakean terms: What prevents such self-reflective activity from collapsing into a Urizenic self-absorption? I take it that this is more or less the same question you (addressing AM) raised earlier.

Blake's answer, reduced to its simplest terms, appeared in that set of activities to which he gave the magical name, Los. This power is Blake's constructive genius, the figure who creates, along with his "sons," the historical world. The maker of this world is named Los because such a world comprises what Blake calls "the perishing . . . Memory" (*Milton* 26:46). The function of Los, in his world of continuous losses, is to carry on a perpetual process of (re)constructions. Los's function is to ensure that not one moment of time or space should fall into "Nonentity." Though he is often called "Imagination," therefore, he is equally the agent of inspired and salvific acts of memory.

I recall Blake's views here because his work helps to clarify the relation between "fact" and imagination.[15] As etymology suggests, a "fact" is something that is made, an artificial construct. From any immediate point of view a fact is the consequence of some particular deed, the locus of an interaction between specific social agencies. Reflexively, "the facts" are those bodies of knowledge which we choose to construct and record in various ways. In Blake's view, therefore, the "facts" of any case are as various as the agents involved in the events, either immediately or belatedly. An extreme factive multiplicity prevails in the immediate moment of human action as well as in the secondary moment of human reflection. This multiplicity, in the context (for example) of contemporary literary studies, is exactly what licenses every move to revise and reimagine the canon. Such revisions become possible when memory is opened to re-membering.

In contrast to De Man, Blake's work throws the burden of authority on energy rather than on reason, on the prolific rather than the devouring, on all those "Minute Particulars" which make up processes of generation and regeneration. The ultimate point of Blake's minute particulars is not so much to create or to "decreate" meaning—although this is most certainly part of what they do—but to establish the grounds on which ideological activity of every kind occurs. More clearly than most, Blake's work foregrounds its own critical and imaginative limits.

From this perspective, hermeneutics is not a science of the "meanings of things"—the blindness/insight dialectic—but a science of the aspects of things, a science not of the way things *are* but of the way they are perceived to be. An anthropological rather than an ontological science—rooted in case studies, "fieldwork," facticities. The historical reconstruction of the text(s) and editions of *Hugh Selwyn Mauberley* should therefore be seen as a model of what hermeneutics entails: the factive revelation of several different frameworks and scales within which that work has been and continues to be constituted.

Nothing illustrates these matters so well as the italic T on page 16 of Pound's work. That T is a "fact" in the sense that it had to be *executed* as what it is, had to be made (*factum*). For the *fact* is that the text could have had a decorated T on this page, that the "supply of Ts" had not in *fact* run out. The italic T is thereby made into an allusion to another (historical) fact about the practice of "old printers"; and that allusion serves as a factive synecdoche for the larger memorial acts which *Hugh Selwyn Mauberley* carries out. In the end, the italic T may well come to stand as an index of the way Pound's work, and poetry in general, *makes* its escape from fiction.

Hermeneutics may of course defend and maintain a work's dominant interpretive inheritances, thereby relegating indomitable and unwarranted claims to obscurity. But if one's interest is in having "the scale of one's attention . . . changed," as you said (speaking to AM), then a materialist and historical literary criticism seems one of the more reliable methods to pursue. After all, the antithetical reading of *Hugh Selwyn Mauberley* which you yourself deployed was only managed because a critical scholarship was able to restore certain aspects of the poem to memory. Critical reflection is nothing but your "mirror of production" without an archive of facts—"facts" understood in the sense I have been discussing. Innocent readers of *Hugh Selwyn Mauberley* confront a transparency when they confront what has been variously called "a text" or "the poem itself." One has to move "from text to work" in order to break free into the particular (dis)orders which works of imagination solicit.

There is a moment in every poem, in every reading of every poem, which Satan's watchfiends cannot find. It is a moment of freedom when the work discovers a door through which it may escape from its own rational inertias. The decorated Ts in Pound's poem are one such moment we may call back to mind. Pound once opened their door, and when scholarship later remembers to reopen it, the act can reimagine the whole work in an entirely new way.

JJR: And let me add that it is the "thickness" of the facticities, the extravagance and even the irrelevance of the detail, which grounds the differential play you speak of. The more a work is materially and historically particularized, the greater the secondary particularity (interpretive and ideological translation) it draws to itself. The many differentials that swirl within *Hugh Selwyn Mauberley*'s fundamental self-contradictions replicate themselves at the interpretive level of the text. Literature is the single house of life which stands only when it *is* divided against itself.

AM: Such a pretty piece of paganism, that last remark. In our day, I suspect even Christians would find it charming. Because it isn't *serious* about its call for literature's self-division. It speaks an ingratiating irony, the wit of accommodation. It might even raise smiles in the halls of academe.

Besides, you both should beware giving lectures on the evils of rationalizing criticism, especially when you have such orderly and authoritative concepts of imaginative fact and memory.

You approve McGann's bibliographical demonstration of one of the hidden histories in *Hugh Selwyn Mauberley*, and you want to accommodate my "antithetical reading" of that hidden history and its relevant facts into your defense of hermeneutics. Well then, tell me what to do with the following (not so hidden) history of the text of Pound's work.

The first poem in the *Hugh Selwyn Mauberley* sequence begins, "For three years, out of key with his time." It appears on page 9 in the Ovid Press edition, where it goes under the title "E. P. ODE POUR LELECTION DE SON SEPULCHRE." In the table

173

of contents of that edition, however, the title is *Ode pour l'election de son sepulchre*. I leave aside the typographical difference between these two titles (small capitals as opposed to italics) even though it is just the sort of apparently irrelevant differential detail which poetry is so apt to exploit. For the titles are skewed in two other, even more dramatic, particulars: first, the table of contents does not begin the title with the initials "E. P."; and second, the roman numeral I is placed *after* the title on page 9.

The work was next printed in Boni and Liveright's American edition of Pound's *Poems 1918–21*, where "E. P." does not appear either on the poem's page title or in the table of contents, and where the roman numeral again appears after the poem's title. Everything changes once again in the work's next printing, the 1926 edition of *Personae* (again, Boni and Liveright). Here the roman numeral from page 9 appears before the poem's title, not after it, and the "E. P." is printed as part of the title in both table of contents and text. All subsequent printings follow this text.

John Espey was the first to notice the textual problem here, and he argued (persuasively, I think) that the physical texts of 1920 and 1921 urged the reader to see a close "identification of Pound and Mauberley."[16] Espey wants to read the sequence so that the two figures are clearly distinguished, and in the case of the first poem to see it as "Ezra Pound's ode" for or about Mauberley (Espey 18). He therefore argues that the final and now dominant text is the correct text in the sense that it is the text which most strongly intimates a clear distinction between Pound and Mauberley.

In fact, the first printing of the "Ode," in *The Dial* of September 1920, also did not print "E. P." as part of the title.[17] Espey regards all the texts of 1920 and 1921 as clear evidence of a "misleading . . . confusion" (Espey 19) in the work which only becomes gradually cleared up in subsequent editions. But one could, of course, equally argue from this textual evidence that Pound might have changed his mind about his own work as he began to see it in print—that he only gradually came to desire "a complete divorce between Pound and Mauberley" (Espey 16).

More than that, one could also argue that the received text still does not by any means make the clear distinction Espey wants. One could read the placement of the initials "E. P." in the title of the "Ode" not as an indication that "E. P." is the author of the ode, but the referent of the noun "son." The introduction of the "E. P.," far from separating Pound from Mauberley, suggests that they are part of the same debased cultural milieu—that "E. P.," in short, is as much a character in Ezra Pound's poetic sequence *Hugh Selwyn Mauberley* as the figure named in the title of the sequence. "E. P." does not simply mean the historical author Ezra Pound.

The texts as we receive them cannot finally decide between these interpretive options. Espey wants to persuade us that the texts of 1920–21 have come about through oversights and "confusion" on the author's part. But in fact the entire textual history—even if we assume that Pound eventually wanted to draw the clear distinction that Espey favors—shows that the work, as it were, randomly and on its own initiative, maintains its ambiguous and unstable features.

Poetry resists rational and clarified orders, whether these be authoritative or hermeneutic. In poems, something there is that cannot love those walls. I am reminded here of Saussure's strange discoveries of the (apparently random) paragrams and anagrams in late Latin verse—in Lucretius's *De rerum natura*, for example, where numerous anagrams of the name Aphrodite continually appear. To Steve McCaffery, these textual phenomena do not emerge "from an intentionality or conscious rhetoricity" but rather seem "an inevitable consequence of writing's alphabetic, combinatory nature":

175

Seen in this way . . . meaning becomes partly the production of a general economy, a persistent excess, non-intentionality and expenditure without reserve through writing's component letters.[18]

I would only add that this kind of "persistent excess" arises not merely from the *letters* of scriptural forms, but from the entire physique of every (and whatever) communicative medium one works in. In all, excess reigns. The facts of a case will not be contained by the interpretations we try to put upon them. Indeed, the interpretations are only other facts disguising themselves as meanings. The word is always and everywhere made flesh.

CONCLUSION

No subject is more fundamental to literary and cultural studies than the subject of "the text."[1] For the past sixty years it has been a central focus of attention for practical scholars and theoreticians alike. Yet to this day no literary topic is more vexed with controversy, or more prone to careless thinking or misrepresentation.

Like cells or thunderstorms (and unlike a triangle, or time), texts are empirical phenomena. Consequently, a theoretical study of them will necessarily be materialist in character and constrained to negotiate itself through the study of highly particular cases. But because texts—like revolutions and families, but unlike cells and thunderstorms—are social rather than natural phenomena, our textual knowledge is deepest when it is most personal and most historical. Once again, therefore, theory of texts cannot move long or far from specific examples and case studies.

People who address themselves to the problem of texts and textuality often point out that the root of the word "text" means "weaving," as in our word "textile." But the problem remains: What is it that is being woven; how is it done?

The Oxford English Dictionary (OED) defines the word "text," in its primary meaning, as follows: "The wording of anything written or printed; the structure formed by the words in their order; the very words, phrases, and sentences as written."

This definition immediately confronts one with the basic paradox of all language: that it is incommensurate with itself, that it cannot mean what it says. The ancients struggled with the paradox under a dialectic they named "verba" and "res," or words and things. Today we know the same paradox by the famous McLuhan distinction between medium and message.

Where is this paradox in the OED definition, you will ask? It appears when you look at the page carrying the definition and then pose the following question: "What is 'the text' of the text represented as being the primary definition of the word 'text'; what is the particular material 'thing' that corresponds to these *ipsa verba*?" Well, in one sense such a "text" has no material existence, for it comprises an abstraction. The "text" in such a view is the *idea* of textuality comprised in the definition. In another sense, however, the definition's "text" is exactly the twenty-four words which make up the primary definition. In yet a third sense the "text" of the passage is the single word, "text," which the twenty-four words in the passage seek to define.

I could easily multiply the difficulties involved here—for example, by inquiring not into the "text" of the OED's definition, but into its meaning. The substantive form of the word "text," for example, is assigned five principal meanings in the OED, and four of these are subdivided into further meanings. I gave the text of the first of these five meanings, but if you examine the OED's "primary meaning" closely you will see that it comprises three distinct statements whose significations overlap, though they do not by any means correspond exactly with each other.

The greatness of the OED partly lies in the way it foregrounds the complications I have been calling attention to. It is famously a dictionary "on Historical Principles," and, as such, it illustrates its "meanings" with multiple examples taken from texts which use or carry the words being defined. In this sense the OED is always reminding us of the Wittgensteinian dictum about words and language in general, that their meaning is to be found in the way they are used. Or as we have more recently learned to say, that the medium is the message.

Like James A. H. Murray (the original compiler of the OED), Wittgenstein was trying to break the spell of a certain idealist theory of language—that words correctly used should correspond to specific things, whether they be concrete things (the word "table" corresponding, for example, to a particular object one writes or eats on) or abstractions (the word "idea," or the word "text," or the word "table" as it may refer to the table-concept). The meaning of the word "text," in such a critical view, will only correspond to the primary definition I originally quoted in a certain loose but relatively general way. That is, it will correspond in (what Wittgenstein called) "the language game" implicitly predicated by the definition itself (which includes the more general language game of making definitions).

Unlike a theory of mathematics, or a theory of cellular development, a theory of texts is difficult to formulate because one fundamental distinction cannot be firmly drawn: that between the subject being studied and the tools by which the study is to be executed. This is a difficult distinction in any case, even in the so-called hard sciences. But in the study of texts the distinction is especially treacherous.

The problem is not simply a matter of trying to match recalcitrant particular cases with inflexible generalities. For example, suppose I do not pose the general question, "What is a text?" but that I ask instead the following very particular question: "What is *this* text?"—that is to say, the text we are involved with right now. Here we seem to be on more firm ground, because this question is a call for an empirical specification—something one can point to, even (perhaps) lay one's hands on. In this case we do not appear even to *enter* that epistemological hall of mirrors raised by the first question I posed. Our new question operates, we might want to say, in the language game of facticity, and ignores the legalistic and merely verbal paradoxes that so fascinated the theological mind of Wittgenstein. Our new question is one a scientist or any practical person can come to grips with.

In the context of this new question, the OED's primary definition may come as a great help rather than a potential stumbling block, for it specifies "this text" as a certain group of words arranged in a certain particular order.

What group of words? Why,—*this* group, *these very words*!

Well, if they are empirical words, then we should be able to locate them, to define their material coordinates. But that need to locate the text, which is an imperative in the language game of facticity, suddenly looms as a serious problem. Let us, for procedural purposes, arbitrarily name the object of our search *this text*, which is no more than the phrase embedded in the initial question, "What is *this* text?" *This text* has a number of possible locations. I begin with only two of them:

1. It is the written order of words on the typescript pages I have in front of me at "this" very moment, and that I "now" hold up before my eyes;[2]

2. It is the oral and spectacular order of words which come to you "now" in the form of a lecture you are partly hearing and partly watching.[3]

These two material orders of words—let us name them typescript and lecture, respectively—are quite different. For one thing, they do not have exactly the same words. If you tape-recorded the lecture, and then compared the words on the tape with the words on the typescript, you would discover numerous variations. But those word variations comprise the least of the differences between the two textual forms. The typescript, for example, has a whole system of scripts which are entirely absent from the lecture you watch and hear—I mean, of course, the punctuation, capitalization, and other diacritical marks that appear all over the typescript. For its part, the lecture comprises semiological forms which are unknown to the typescript: my gestures, my intonations, the present institutional context, and so forth. Indeed, the "order of the words" is in each case not at all the same: the lecture phrasings necessarily define word orders which do not correspond to those we might define through an analysis of the grammar and rhetoric of the typescript.

But the problem grows more complex the further we look into it. Suppose I were to deliver *this text* as a lecture next month, when I shall be in Chicago. Clearly, if *that* lecture were taped, it would vary once again, both from the typescript I have before me and from the lecture we all here remain in the midst of, and which might be taped, if I ever get to the end of it. And every time I give the lecture again, the elementary order of the words will also vary. As the Eastern philosopher said of his interpretive turtles, it is variation all the way down.

But, we might imagine, at least the typescript will keep its integrity and remain equal to itself. Alas, we must come to see that even this is not the case. For the typescript, like the lecture, is a certain kind of human construct, and hence it cannot be objectively situated (whether by rational definition or by scientific description). Its own radical particularity forbids such permanence and commensurability. In the first place, the typescript has inscribed within it an entire production history comprising numerous changes and variations. Furthermore, as a certain type of communicative mechanism the typescript, like the lecture, is the locus of human intercourse. Every time this typescript is put to some communicative use, it undergoes transformation.

Think back for a moment to Murray's Oxford English Dictionary and its method of illustrating its various definitions by giving examples from actual texts where the words being defined originally appeared. When the dictionary lays out its illustrative passages, all the quoted texts are placed in an entirely new frame of reference—that is, they are framed into their new function(s) as part of the Oxford English Dictionary. In the dictionary, the words being defined—specifically, the words in the exemplary passages—do not mean what they mean in the (original) texts from which they have been drawn.

A similar instability inhabits every text, including (as my thought frames itself) "this typescript." When the typescript is used, for example, as the basis for a lecture (like this one), the typescript is—as we have seen—radically transformed. If I used the typescript as my point of departure for another lecture, you may be certain that I would make material changes in the typescript. Or if I used the typescript as the basis (what textual scholars call the copy-text) for printing *this text* somewhere, say in a Blakean "book, that all may read,"[4] I would make other alterations. Besides, as soon as *this text* moves from typescript form to printed form, it undergoes drastic kinds of new variation. And if it were, like Shakespeare's *Hamlet* or Newton's *Principia*, retransmitted repeatedly in a wild variety of different forms, times, and circumstances—in many printed venues, in lectures and conversations, on stage—the alterations in *this text* might unsettle even the imagination of Jorge Luis Borges.

All texts are subject to change and, ultimately, to final destruction. We do not have the texts of Homer, we have only texts which recollect his (if he *was* a single person) original (oral) performances, and those scriptural texts are separated from Homer and his world by vast stretches of place, time, and circumstance. Our received Homeric texts are, at best, Alexandrian residues. The bible itself, the word of God, comes to us in vessels we know to be corrupt and broken. Since the eighteenth century, when the sciences of archaeology, ethnography, and anthropology were first imagined, we have been trying to arrest these processes of change and to preserve intact the originality of whatever we encounter or study. Vain as the endeavor must be, from a scientific point of view, it has been immensely fruitful. Lost in the past, originality blossoms again, like spring, which "breeding flowers, will never breed the same."

Properly understood, *this text*, every text, is unique and original to itself when we consider it not as an object but as an action. That is to say, *this text* is always a new (and changed) originality each time it is textually engaged. Suppose *this text* came to be regarded the way we regard, for example, the Constitution of the United States, or the Bill of Rights, or as the English regard the Magna Charta. *This text* would be worked over by skilled technicians in order to save it from the ordinary ravages of time. Its typescript (which is one form of *this text*) would be put under special glass, perhaps set out on public display, and it would be reproduced in countless ways, including the facsimiles we might buy in stores and gift shops. Could we not then say that *this text* had at last been preserved from change? So, I might finish this lecture, and a scholar might come and wisk away my typescript and immediately hand it over to the keeping of the preservationists who work in the Library of Congress; another scholar might have made a videotape and turn that text over to another group of preservationists. (But what if two videotapes were made, necessarily from different points of view? Of course the scholars would try to preserve both and would carefully note—or try to note—all the differences between the two. They would fail in this endeavor, naturally.)

This typescript preserved in the Library of Congress, that (or those) videotape(s) protected with equal care, will not be the same as their originals—any more than our Bill of Rights under glass or sold in gift shop facsimiles is the same as the original document executed toward the end of the eighteenth century. All of these texts may have (virtually) the same *linguistic* constitution, may even have, to a certain varying degree, similar or analogous *bibliographical* forms. Nonetheless, all are different, radically so. *This* typescript preserved in the Library of Congress is not at all the same as *this* typescript which lies before me now because the linguistic text, in each case, will have been socially constituted in utterly different ways. (Let me also point out that *this* typescript lying before me itself varies from its electronic (word processed) base text, and from the printout of that electronic text which I generated—several times.) Texts are always linked to contexts—are, in fact, the chief means we have of understanding and reengaging contexts.

Such differentials between otherwise "identical" linguistic texts usually arise to our consciousness in the form of different interpretations—that is to say, in the form of other texts which we generate in order to specify or define the "meaning" of earlier textual sites. Everyone agrees, of course, that meaning is a wild variable, but people also commonly assume that the "originals" do not vary, or (perhaps) that they vary at a much slower rate. Once the words are set down on the page, we imagine them as fixed for good—always understanding, of course, that physical deterioration may erode such fixity over time. In this view we see texts as relatively stable, whereas interpretation is sowing the wind.

But the fact is that interpretation is an act which gets carried out only as a response to a given textual condition. We say that two interpreters of a particular text "read" it differently because they are not seeing the same "text," because they have imagined their interpretive object differently. In our own day, these interpretive differentials are ordinarily ascribed (inscribed) to the authority of readers, who make meanings according to what they imagine to be most interesting or useful or marketable. The meanings, in this scenario, are imagined to originate in readers, who translate and reimagine the passive texts that come under their hands.

This fairly recent way of thinking about meaning has displaced altogether the common, earlier way. The latter conceived the interpreter as one who set out in quest of *the* meaning of the text. Interpretive variation, in such a case, need not be a sign of the interpreter's constructive or creative activity (though it *could* be that); rather, it signalled, characteristically, the failure of the reader to penetrate to the whole truth of the text. The extreme variability of midrashic interpretations of the bible is the (paradoxical) sign of this approach to reading a text: the Word of God is One, like its Truth, though the words of men are many, like themselves.

Let me point out, however, that in each of these interpretive theories, the stability of the material *text*—the interpretive location, or material object—is assumed.

On the contrary, however, what I am arguing here is that no such stability in the material object can be assumed with respect to texts. (In scientific enquiry itself, insofar as an atom, or a quark, or a superstring is a *text*, they must be assumed to be variables in their own textual fields, just as those textual fields themselves must be judged as variables within the larger textual field—the language game—we call science.)[5] If we define a text as words in a certain order, then we have to say that the ordering of the words in every text is *in fact*, at the factive level, unstable. No text, either conceptually or empirically, can have the "ordering of its words" defined or specified as invariant.

Variation, in other words, is the invariant rule of the textual condition. Interpretive differentials (or the freedom of the reader) are not the origin or cause of the variation, they are only its most manifest set of symptoms.

Some might fear that such a theory of the radical instability of the material and conceptual "text" would lead to intellectual anarchy and the collapse of the possibility of a reliable knowledge of texts. But in truth, only from such a theoretical position can one begin to imagine the possibility of reliable knowledge. Such knowledge, however, as in Murray's great dictionary, will be knowledge imagined and transmitted "on historical principles." This is true because every text—

whether it be a printed book, a conversation, any type of natural phenomenon, whatever—localizes human temporalities. To the interpreter, texts often appear as images of time; to the maker of texts, however, they are the very events of time and history itself.

Notes

INTRODUCTION

1. Paul De Man, "The Rhetoric of Blindness," in *Blindness and Insight: Essays in the Rhetoric of Contemporary Criticism*, with an introduction by Wlad Godzich (Minneapolis: University of Minnesota Press, 1983), 107.

2. "Variations on Authority: Some Deconstructive Transformations of the New Criticism," in *The Yale Critics: Deconstruction in America*, eds. Jonathan Arac, Wlad Godzich, Wallace Martin (Minneapolis: University of Minnesota Press, 1983), 7–11.

3. G. Thomas Tanselle, *A Rationale of Textual Criticism* (Philadelphia: University of Pennsylvania Press, 1989), 64–65.

4. Percy Bysshe Shelley, "A Defence of Poetry," in *Shelley's Prose, or the Trumpet of a Prophecy*, ed. David Lee Clark (Albuquerque: University of New Mexico Press, 1954), 294.

5. Shelley's elegiac idealism, which I have thus far emphasized, stands in sharp contrast to his (parallel and contradictory) impulses to celebrate the perfection of poetry and the mortal world. Just prior to his lament over the waning of inspiration in "A Defence of Poetry," for example, he speaks of poetry as "the perfect and consummate surface and bloom of all things; it is as the odor and the color of the rose to the texture of the elements which compose it" (293).

6. Note that this alternative view of perfection makes allowance for *im*perfections—those true flaws and cripplings which all things human stand in danger of.

7. For McLaverty's approach to the problems raised by this question see his "The Mode of Existence of Literary Works of Art: The Case of the *Dunciad* Variorum," *Studies in Bibliography* 37 (1984): 82–105. See also Peter L. Shillingsburg, "Text as Matter, Concept, and Action," ibid. 44 (1991): 31–82.

8. I am appropriating the mathematical term "Chaotic Order" and applying it to textual conditions, where it seems to me an ex-

tremely useful concept. See Heinz-Otto Peitgen and Peter H. Richter, *The Beauty of Fractals* (Berlin: Springer-Verlag, 1986); and for a lively historical survey, James Gleick, *Chaos. Making a New Science* (New York: Viking, 1987).

9. See Humberto Maturana and Francisco Varela, *Autopoiesis and Cognition: The Realization of the Living* (Dordrecht, Holland: D. Reidel, 1980), and *The Biological Roots of Human Understanding*, trans. Robert Paolucci (Boston and London: New Science Library, Shambhala, 1988).

10. See Genette's remarks about paratextual "manifestations . . . purement factuelles." Gérard Genette, *Seuils* (Paris: Editions de Seuil, 1987), 12–13.

CHAPTER 1

1. The allusion here is to Paul DeMan, *The Resistance to Theory* (Minneapolis: University of Minnesota Press, 1986).

2. A good introduction to literary pragmatics is *Literary Pragmatics*, ed. Roger D. Sell (London and New York: Routledge, 1991).

3. That is to say, in the period when Anglo-American literary studies were experiencing a strong and widespread turn to theoretical studies in general.

4. A good introduction to the revolution in Shakespearean textual studies is Gary Taylor and Michael Warren, eds., *The Division of the Kingdoms: Shakespeare's Two Versions of King Lear* (Oxford: Oxford University Press, 1983).

5. William Michael Rossetti's first edition of the poems appeared in 1886. He reprinted it several times, augmenting it in 1904 and again, more comprehensively, in 1911.

6. I sketch an answer to this question in "Dante Gabriel Rossetti, or the Truth Betrayed," in *Towards a Literature of Knowledge* (Oxford and Chicago: Oxford University Press and University of Chicago Press, 1989), especially pp. 79–85.

7. "Natural" because of my long association with the press, and because of their interest in producing critical editions of English authors.

8. This is no small supposition in itself, as one may see very clearly in the case of imagining a possible edition of Ezra Pound; or

even in the case of the current edition from Garland of the younger romantics. The editing of Byron, in the Garland series, is subject to certain constraints and limitations because of restrictions on the use of original manuscript materials. See, for example, Alice Levine and Jerome J. McGann eds., *The Manuscripts of the Younger Romantics: Byron*, 4 vols. (New York: Garland, 1986–1988).

9. I refer to this work henceforth with the abbreviation *HL*.

10. In this discussion one might reasonably take my question "What is a text?" to be a sociological and a historical question *rather than* a philosophical and ontological one. In the context of a materialist pragmatics, however, the distinction between sociological/historical questions, and philosophical/ontological ones, is itself understood as a sociohistorical distinction. The distinction is therefore highly problematic, and—in my view—can only be made in the full consciousness that it is not an ontological distinction. It is (or can be) a "philosophical" distinction if "philosophy" is understood as the history of certain social practices, and if it is pursued within the consciousness of that horizon of practices.

11. Paull F. Baum, ed., *The House of Life: A Sonnet Sequence by Dante Gabriel Rossetti* (Cambridge: Harvard University Press, 1928); Cecil Y. Lang, ed., *The Pre-Raphaelites and Their Circle* (Boston: Houghton Mifflin, 1968).

12. I have not seen this edition, but it is noted and discussed in William E. Fredeman, "Rossetti's 'In Memoriam': An Elegiac Reading of *The House of Life*," *Bulletin of the John Rylands Library* 47 (March 1965): 299n. What Copeland and Day allude to in their promotion of their edition is the fact that *HL* at one time—in particular, in 1870—had been printed by Rossetti in a form which had included these eleven songs. Like 6a, however, these songs were removed by Rossetti when he printed the 102-sonnet *HL* in 1881. When Copeland and Day restore the songs, they represent their act as giving the work in its "full text" for "the first time." This is no misrepresentation, though it is also not "the truth." Copeland and Day are simply mistaken about what constitutes (or what might constitute) the "full text" of *HL*.

13. For a good schedule of these printings see Fredeman, especially pp. 336–41.

14. This manuscript version was printed in 1954 in an (unsatisfactory) edition: see John Robert Wahl, ed., *The Kelmscott Love*

Sonnets of Dante Gabriel Rossetti (Cape Town: A. A. Balkema, 1954), 3–33.

15. For a further treatment of these distinctions see my *Social Values and Poetic Acts* (Cambridge: Harvard University Press, 1988), 260–61 n28.

16. This book was reprinted in 1971 under yet another title, *The Oxford Book of English Verse of the Romantic Period, 1798–1837*. These changing titles exhibit the chief problem I am discussing here. Milford was keenly aware of the problem, as the following remark from his 1928 preface shows: "The title [of this book] is unsatisfactory. It is, however, convenient, intelligible, and easily remembered; and if the poets—except the satirists—and the Regency had little to do with one another, yet the head of the State during most of the period was the Prince Regent, and the book may be fairly named from the top of its chronological arch" (viii).

17. Note that the first of these books is printed in Edinburgh (i.e., outside of England), the second is privately printed, and the last appears through the regular trade (Longman), first with a Bristol imprint (1798), and second with a London (1800). These elementary bibliographical matters are highly significant for the meaning of each of these works, both in themselves and in the context of literary history as well.

18. See J. T. Mathias's *The Pursuits of Literature*, the first part of which appeared in 1794.

19. At this writing two titles are favored: the one just given, and *The New Oxford Book of Verse: The Romantic Age, 1785–1830*.

20. Analogous course protocols have to be followed for larger graduate as well as for undergraduate classes. This is not the context, however, for discussing these related pedagogical scenes.

21. The distinction here means to recall the influential Demanian diad "blindness and insight." For a more detailed critique of DeMan's dialectical concept see Jerome McGann, *Social Values and Poetric Acts*, 1–5, 101–11.

CHAPTER 2

1. See Jerome J. McGann, *A Critique of Modern Textual Criticism* (Chicago: University of Chicago Press, 1983); "The Monks

and the Giants: Textual and Bibliographical Studies and the Interpretation of Literary Works" and "Shall These Bones Live?", both reprinted in *The Beauty of Inflections: Literary Investigations in Historical Method and Theory* (Oxford: Clarendon Press, 1985), 69–110.

2. The handbook is written by William Proctor Williams and Craig S. Abbott (New York: Modern Language Association of America, 1985).

3. See especially chapter 5, pp. 54–60.

4. *The Poems of Matthew Arnold*, ed. Kenneth Allott (London: Longman, 1965).

5. For a detailed study of these matters see my "Matthew Arnold and the Critical Spirit: The Three Texts of *Empedocles on Etna*," in *Victorian Connections*, ed. Jerome J. McGann (Charlottesville: University Press of Virginia, 1989), 146–71.

6. *The Poems of Matthew Arnold*, ed. H. S. Milford, with an introduction by A. C. Quiller-Couch (London: Oxford University Press, 1909).

7. New and revised edition, with commentary by Harold Bloom (Berkeley and Los Angeles: University of California Press, 1982).

8. The facsimile is taken from the Trianon Press facsimile edition of Copy B of *Jerusalem* (London, 1974).

9. For one detailed examination of the edition's problems see the Santa Cruz Study Group's review in *Blake: An Illustrated Quarterly* 18 (Summer 1984): 4–31.

10. For a detailed presentation of this work along the lines sketched here, see my "Lord Byron and the Truth in Masquerade" (forthcoming in a collection of essays on Byron edited by Alice Levine).

11. See, for example, Peter L. Shillingsburg, *Scholarly Editing in the Computer Age* (Athens: University of Georgia Press, 1986): "Jerome McGann's social contract theory of works of literary art . . . rejects the notion of final authorial intention as an operative factor in textual criticism" (31). See also G. Thomas Tanselle, "Historicism and Critical Editing, 1979–85," in *Textual Criticism Since Greg: A Chronicle 1950–1985* (Charlottesville: University Press of Virginia, 1987), especially pp. 127–35.

12. See *Critique*, 104–5, 121–23.

13. For further details see Richard J. Finneran, *Editing Yeats's Poems* (London: Macmillan, 1983), especially the Prolegomena and chapters 1 and 5.

14. This edition was edited by Noel Polk for Random House (New York, 1986).

15. In an excellent (unpublished) paper "The Unending of *Absalom, Absalom!*" Michael Millgate exposes the problems raised by Noel Polk's decisions to change certain "incorrect" dates in Faulkner's novel (both the main text and the appended chronology). Polk imagines his changes to be simple textual "corrections," but Millgate shows that they interfere with an important other imagination of the novel and its chronological details (an imagination that might even have been "intentional" on Faulkner's part)! Millgate's discussion shows how Polk's scholarly edition itself has become part of the "unending" of Faulkner's book.

16. See Ted-Larry Pebworth, "John Donne, Coterie Poetry, and the Text as Performance," *Studies in English Literature* 29 (Winter 1989): 61–75.

CHAPTER 3

1. Tanselle here is quoting with approval the words of Nicolas Barker. See G. Thomas Tanselle "The Editing of Historical Documents," reprinted from *Studies in Bibliography* (1978) in *Selected Studies in Bibliography* (Charlottesville: University Press of Virginia, 1979), 454.

2. Hershel Parker, *Flawed Texts and Verbal Icons: Literary Authority in American Fiction* (Evanston: Northwestern University Press, 1984), 49.

3. Peter Stoicheff detailed the complex history of the *Drafts and Fragments* text in a lecture at the Yale conference on editing Pound, sponsored by Yale and the Beinecke Library in October, 1989. The lecture forms part of a book which is now in press.

4. John Kidd's recently published "An Inquiry into *Ulysses: The Corrected Text*" supplies, in great detail, the case against the edition in this respect. See *The Papers of the Bibliographical Society of America* 82 (December 1988): 412–584.

5. See Gordon N. Ray, *The Illustrator and the Book in England*

from 1790 to 1914 (New York and Oxford: The Pierpont Morgan Library and Oxford University Press, 1976), 75.

6. See *Vanity Fair by William Makepeace Thackeray*, edited with an introduction by Geoffrey and Kathleen Tillotson (Boston: Houghton Mifflin Co., 1963); see pp. xxii and 80.

7. Gordon Ray, op. cit., xxxix.

8. *Hard Times* was first published in weekly parts in *Household Words* over five months, beginning 1 April 1854. It was then published separately.

9. See *Charles Dickens: Oliver Twist*, ed. Kathleen Tillotson (Oxford: Oxford University Press, 1966), especially pp. 369–71.

10. For the story of these events see Robert L. Patten, *Charles Dickens and His Publishers* (Oxford: Oxford University Press, 1978), chapter 3, especially pp. 63–68.

11. The sepulchral implication of the word "tome" needs no comment. "The white cube" is the phrase made famous by Brian O'Doherty's excellent book *Inside the White Cube: The Ideology of Gallery Space* (Santa Monica and San Francisco: Lapis Press, 1986). The essays in O'Doherty's book first appeared in 1976 in *Artforum*, in slightly different form.

12. "Context as Content" is the title of O'Doherty's third and final section of his book.

13. (Cambridge: Harvard University Press, 1988). See especially chapter 10, "On Collecting Art and Culture."

14. (Chicago: University of Chicago Press, 1983).

15. See *The Poems of Emily Dickinson*, ed. Thomas H. Johnson, 2 vols. (Cambridge: Harvard University Press, 1955); *The Manuscript Books of Emily Dickinson*, ed. R. W. Franklin, 2 vols. (Cambridge: Harvard University Press, 1981).

16. But see Susan Howe's groundbreaking essay on Dickinson in *Sulfur* 28 (1991), 134–55.

CHAPTER 5

1. Mortimer Adler, *How to Read a Book* (New York, 1940), 18.

2. For a good discussion of contemporary reading theories and the crucial choice of emphases (decoding versus constructing), see Gregory G. Colomb, "Cultural Literacy and the Theory of Mean-

ing: Or, What Educational Theorists Need to Know about How We Read," *New Literary History* 20 (Winter 1989): 411–50.

3. Ezra Pound, *ABC of Reading* (New Haven: Yale University Press, 1934), 44, 28–29.

4. Ibid., 32.

5. Pre-Raphaelite decorative traditions, which the early cantos allude to and invoke, are themselves located squarely in the tradition of pictorial abstraction which the twentieth century has pursued so resolutely. Pre-Raphaelite pictures are illusions of representations—"quoted" representations; their highly decorative and ornate surface features disrupt the integrity of the images and call attention to the medium. More than anything else, in fact, Pre-Raphaelite art carries out a disguised attack upon the conventions of pictorial representation.

6. The text here and in the subsequent illustrations from Pound's *Cantos* is from the (1986) reprinting of the New Directions edition of *The Cantos of Ezra Pound*.

7. See Roy Wagner, *Symbols That Stand for Themselves* (Chicago: University of Chicago Press, 1986).

8. The best treatments of this subject in relation to early modern writing are Marjorie Perloff's *The Futurist Moment: Avant Garde, Avant Guerre, and the Language of Rupture* (Chicago: University of Chicago Press, 1986); see also Willard Bohn, *The Aesthetics of Visual Poetry 1914–1928* (Cambridge: Cambridge University Press, 1986).

9. See Ron Silliman, *The New Sentence* (New York: Roof Books, 1987), especially section 2.

10. The date of 1892 in Yeats's title is a complex signal which associates Pater's famous Mona Lisa text, the death of Tennyson, and Yeats's own involvement with the Rhymers Club in the early 1890s. The Mona Lisa passage was first published in *The Renaissance* in 1873, but its importance for Yeats lay in the influence it had on the poets of the 1890s, and beyond them on modern poetry generally. The new generation of poets, for Yeats, stood on the other side of Victorian poetry, for which Tennyson was the symbol. Pater, on the other hand, was for Yeats the inaugurating spiritual force for modern poetry. For related discussions see Jon Stallworthy, "Yeats as Anthologist," in *In Excited Reverie: A Centen-*

ary Tribute to W. B. Yeats 1865–1939, eds. A. Norman Jeffares and K.G.W. Cross (London: Macmillan, 1965), 171–92; Harold Bloom, *Yeats* (New York: Oxford University Press, 1970), chap. 2; and Leonard Nathan, "W. B. Yeats's Experiments with an Influence," *Victorian Studies* 6 (1962): 66–74.

11. I am thinking of the traditional work of G. Thomas Tanselle and Fredson Bowers; see especially Trevor Howard-Hill's defense of this tradition in the forthcoming volume of *Text*, vol. 5.

12. See my "Theory of Texts," *London Review of Books* (18 February 1988): 20–21.

13. I am grateful to Paul Wellen for helping me to understand the conventional representation of Chinese forms.

14. The symmetry is to an analogue and not a digital computer. The distinction is important because, in recent years, so much literacy theory has had recourse to the operations of digital computing. See, for example, the recent enthusiastic essay by Richard Lanham, "The Electronic Word: Literary Study and the Digital Revolution," *New Literary History* 20 (Winter 1989): 265–90; and William Paulson, *The Noise of Culture: Literary Texts in a World of Information* (Ithaca: Cornell University Press, 1988).

15. For a good introduction to the nineteenth-century tradition of this subject see Gordon N. Ray, *The Illustrator and the Book in England from 1790 to 1914* (New York and Oxford: The Pierpont Morgan Library and Oxford University Press, 1976).

16. See John Sutherland, *Bestsellers: Popular Fiction of the 1970s* (London: Routledge and Kegan Paul, 1981).

17. Lawrence Rainey, "The Price of Modernism: Publishing *The Waste Land*," in Ronald Bush, ed. *T. S. Eliot: The Modernist in History* (Cambridge: Cambridge University Press, 1991), 91–133.

CHAPTER 6

1. *Literary Essays*, ed. T. S. Eliot (New York: New Directions, 1968), 86.

2. See "The *Cantos* of Ezra Pound, the Truth in Contradiction," in *Towards a Literature of Knowledge* (Oxford: Oxford University Press, 1989), chap. 4.

3. There is a problem with respect to these cantos because the

decorated editions display two distinct sequences (1–16, 17–27). The unit 1–30 does not come into existence until later, in 1930; and when it does, the initial distinction (1–16, 17–27) is removed. A critical edition of the *Cantos* will have to make some difficult decisions about how to present these texts.

4. For a clear presentation of the lines of disagreement see Bowers's presidential address to the STS, "Unfinished Business," *Text* 4, ed. D. C. Greetham and W. Speed Hill (New York: AMS Press, 1988): 1–11 (especially p. 8) and my paper "The Textual Condition," ibid., 29–37 (included in this book as chapter 4).

5. In his famous "The Application of Thought to Textual Criticism," *Proceedings of the Classical Association* XVIII (1921): 67–84.

6. In conversation with me Lawrence Rainey pointed out (a) that the use of roman numerals was a common fascist practice, and (b) that the dust jacket of the 1933 edition displays the Xs as the leather thongs binding a fasces.

7. This tendency toward productive comprehensiveness may be seen, in one respect, as a feature of the authoritarianism of the modernist approach. However, to the extent that Pound, like Yeats, drew upon the work of William Morris and the legacy of the Kelmscott Press for his interest in the physical presentation of texts, Pound's work here can be connected to Victorian socialist ideals of medieval-artisanal cooperative production. See my essay "Thing to Mind: The Materialist Aesthetic of William Morris," forthcoming in *Huntington Library Quarterly*.

8. I refer to the series of articles Pound published in *The New Age* between 7 December 1911 and 15 February 1912 under the general heading "I Gather the Limbs of Osiris"; this eleven-part sequence is reprinted as Part I of Pound's *Selected Prose 1909–1965*, ed. William Cookson (London: Faber and Faber, 1973), 19–44.

9. For a good discussion of Pound's vorticism which has a bearing on my argument here, see Hugh Kenner, *The Pound Era* (Berkeley and Los Angeles: University of California Press, 1971), 238.

10. For an excellent discussion of Morris and his projects in decorative printing see Norman Kelvin, "Patterns in Time: The

Decorative and the Narrative in the Work of William Morris," in *Nineteenth-Century Lives: Essays Presented to Jerome Hamilton Buckley*, eds. Lockridge, Maynard, and Stone (Cambridge: Cambridge University Press, 1989), 140–68. See also Henry Halliday Sparling's classic *The Kelmscott Press and William Morris Master-Craftsman* (London: Macmillan, 1924). Pound's initial serious involvement with Morris and his ideas must have been while he was working with A. R. Orage and *The New Age*, for whom Morris was a central intellectual resource. See Tim Redman, *Ezra Pound and Fascism* (Cambridge and New York: Cambridge University Press, 1990), chap. 1, especially pp. 21–22.

11. See Joan Friedman's *Color Printing in England 1486–1870* (New Haven: Yale Center for British Art, 1978); Ruari McLean, *Victorian Book Design and Color Printing* (London: Faber and Faber, 1963).

12. See William E. Fredeman, "Emily Faithfull and the Victoria Press: An Experiment in Sociological Bibliography," *The Library*, 5th series, XXIX no. 2 (June 1974): 139–64.

13. After Morris's Kelmscott Press, the Yeatses' venture with the Cuala Press, and the Bodley Head, were the most notable outlets for finely printed work by contemporary writers.

14. For Morris's bibliographical vision and program see *The Ideal Book: Essays and Lectures on the Arts of the Book by William Morris*, ed. William S. Peterson (Berkeley and Los Angeles: University of California Press, 1982).

15. The one distinctive feature of the Kelmscott Press format which Pound's early decorative books did *not* follow was Morris's tight arrangement of words and lines. Kelmscott Press texts are hard to read. The style of modernist decorative books, like Pound's, tended to lead out the lines and, in general, to deliver the text on a page that provided generous spacing throughout.

16. See Vincent De Luca, "A Wall of Words: The Sublime as Text," in *Unnam'd Forms*, eds. Nelson Hilton and Thomas A. Vogler (Berkeley and Los Angeles: University of California Press, 1986), 218–41.

17. Douglas C. McMurtrie, *The Book: The Story of Printing and Bookmaking*, 3rd rev. ed. (Oxford: Oxford University Press, 1943), 460.

18. For an interesting discussion of the promotional and economic factors which contributed to the "anti-Kelmscott" approach to text layout in fine book production in the 1890s and afterwards, see R. D. Brown, "The Bodley Head Press: Some Bibliographical Extrapolations," *Papers of the Bibliographical Society of America* 61 (1967): 39–50.

19. In his visual treatment of the page Pound is in certain respects closer to Blake than he is to Morris. Both Blake and Pound treat the page as an integral unit, whereas for Morris the visual bibliographical unit was not the "page" but the "opening" (i.e., the two pages that appear together when a book is opened to view). See *The Ideal Book*, 64–65, 70–71.

20. Cantos 72–73 were first issued not through a commercial printing institution, but through an ideological one, an organ of fascist propaganda.

21. I am grateful to Paul Wellen for helping me to understand Pound's appropriation of these Western conventions for representing the acoustic dimension of Chinese characters.

22. In the finished typescripts of Canto CX the word appears at the bottom on the second typed page.

23. My Rossetti texts are all taken from *The Works of Dante Gabriel Rossetti*, ed. William Michael Rossetti (London: Ellis, 1911).

CHAPTER 7

1. The date of 1862 is probably most significant, for it was then that Christina Rossetti's *Goblin Market* volume was published, with a title page ornament by her brother, and decorated covers, also designed by D. G. Rossetti. From that point on Rossetti, Morris, and Burne-Jones became increasingly concerned about book production and design. For good introductory treatments of these subjects see Douglas McMurtrie, *The Book: The Story of Printing and Bookmaking* (Oxford: Oxford University Press, 1937), chaps. 32–36; Ruari McLean, *Victorian Book Design and Color Printing* (London: Faber and Faber, 1963).

2. See G. Thomas Tanselle, "Textual Criticism and Literary Sociology," *Studies in Bibliography* 44 (1991): 87, 90, 112.

3. See *Poetry* II (April 1913): 12. All subsequent printings give the poem in its received (and conventional) typographical form.

4. Pound's directions to the printer show the clear influence of William Morris's ideas about page design, especially on the matter of the margins; see Morris's two papers "Printing" and "The Ideal Book," reprinted in *The Ideal Book. Essays and Lectures on the Arts of the Book by William Morris*, ed. William S. Peterson (Berkeley and Los Angeles: University of California Press, 1982), especially pp. 64–65, 70–71.

5. Once again the influence of Morris appears, this time in Pound's phrase "the old printers" (see ibid.).

6. Catherine Gallagher, "Marxism and the New Historicism," in *The New Historicism*, ed. H. Aram Veeser (New York: Routledge, 1989), 45.

7. See Stanley Fish's "Commentary: The Young and the Restless," which concludes and reflects upon the various essays in Veeser's collection *The New Historicism* (pp. 303–16).

8. See Roberto Unger's *False Necessity* (Cambridge: Cambridge University Press, 1987), the second volume of his three part *Politics, a Work in Constructive Social Theory*.

9. See Roland Barthes's famous essay (first published in *Revue d'esthetique*), reprinted and translated in his *Image-Music-Text*, ed. and trans. Stephen Heath (London: Fontana, 1977).

10. The allusion here is to my "The Text, the Poem, and the Problem of Historical Method," reprinted in *The Beauty of Inflections: Literary Essays in Historical Method and Theory* (Oxford: Oxford University Press, 1985), 111–32.

11. The two 1920 texts are *The Dial*'s initial printing of the first six sections of the poem and the Ovid Press edition. In 1921 Boni and Liveright brought out the first American edition, in 1926 the first edition of *Personae* printed the poem again, with changes, and further changes were made in the 1949 printing of *Personae*. A few more changes were made, with Pound's authority, when John Espey printed a text of the work in his important study *Ezra Pound's Mauberley*.

12. See Jean Baudrillard, *The Mirror of Production*, trans. Mark Poster (St. Louis: Telos Press, 1975).

13. What Mack says here recalls the general argument in

Baudrillard's *De la seduction* (Paris: Galilee, 1979), recently published in English as *Seduction*, trans. Brian Singer (New York: St. Martin's Press, 1990).

14. See Paul De Man, *Blindness and Insight: Essays in Rhetoric and Contemporary Criticism*, 2nd revised ed., introduction by Wlad Godzich (Minneapolis: University of Minnesota Press, 1983), 19.

15. It is commonly believed that Blake's commitment to "Imagination" entailed a reciprocal hostility to fact. This view is quite wrong. What Blake wanted to free poetry from was what he called "morals," which is his term for what we would call "meanings" and "interpretations." See my "William Blake Illuminates the Truth," in *Towards a Literature of Knowledge* (Oxford: Oxford University Press, 1989), chap. 1.

16. See John Espey, *Ezra Pound's Mauberley: A Study in Composition* (Berkeley and Los Angeles: University of California Press, 1955, 1974), 19.

17. *The Dial* text prints the first six poems from Part I of the sequence: see vol. LXIX, no. 3, pp. [283]-87.

18. Steve McCaffery, "Writing as a General Economy," in *North of Intention: Critical Writings 1973–1986* (New York: Roof Books, 1986), 208.

CONCLUSION

1. The first public constitution of this text was as a lecture at University of Nevada (Las Vegas) in 1990. The text here is a printed version of that lecture.

2. Let it be noted that this "first state" is self-incommensurate: for the production of the typescript necessarily passed through a great many different constitutions from its first drafting on my word processor.

3. I have retained the distinction I made originally, even though the immediate format—this published book—comprises yet another textual condition. Indeed, for my purposes this third general state simply underscores the point I want to establish.

4. See Blake's "Introduction" to *Songs of Innocence*.

5. It is a deep philosophical problem in science whether the material order of things should be regarded as a text (in the sense I am using the term here) or as a pretextual "reality." Are the incommensurates of quantum mechanics a function of our mathematical tools, or are they "real?" Philosophers of science differ sharply over this question.

Index

203